Kotzebue, 1951.

MR. ALASKA
The Chuck West Story
Sixty Years of Alaska Tourism
From Bush Pilot to Patriarch

Third Edition

Charles B. West

Weslee Publishing
SEATTLE, WASHINGTON **2005**

I want to acknowledge the help of Bob Davis in preparing this book for publication. Without his time and skills, it would never have been possible. CBW.

Library of Congress Cataloging in Publication Data.

West, Charles B., 1914-
  Mr. Alaska — the Chuck West Story

  1. West, Charles B., 1914-   2. Travel Agents
Alaska — Biography   I. Title.
G154.5.WA7A33 1985   917.98'045   85-50666

Published by Weslee Publishing,
Copyright © 2005 Charles B. West

Manufactured by McNaughton & Gunn

ISBN 978-0-933319-00-2

To Marguerite, my wife and companion of 60 years.

and to our children: CarraLee
Barbara
Charles
Richard
Ral

and our grandchildren: James Mitchell Fausey
Kyler Carter West
John Douglas Bolger
Juliane Marie Fausey/Harris
Thomas Richard Bolger
Joseph Edward Bolger
Michael Richard West
Brittana Lee West Hardwick
Zachary Eugene West
Lauren Ashley West
Charles Ryan West
Makena Marie West Hardwick

And our great grandchildren: Callie Marie Fausey
Joseph Mitchell Fausey
Makai J Harris
Kiele Marie Harris
Carter Liam West
Dillon Bryce West
John-Thomas Joseph Bolger
Ethan Lucas West

and those to come.

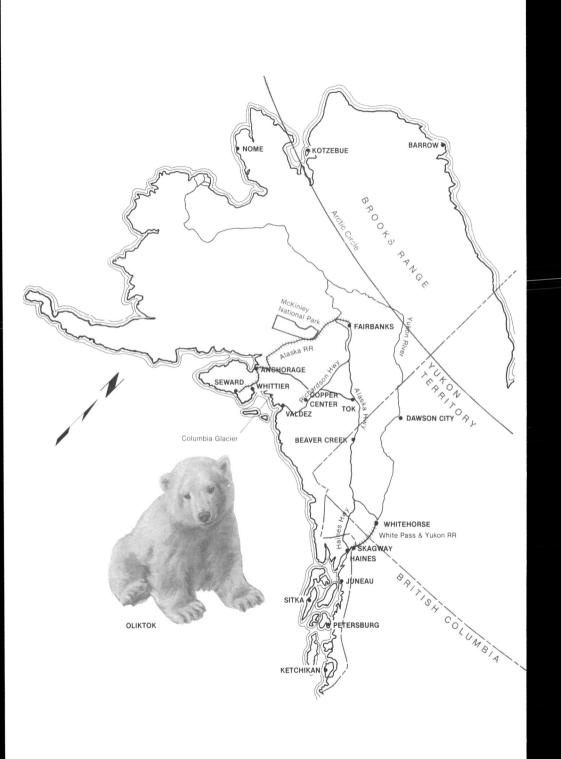

NOME

KOTZEBUE

BARROW

BROOKS RANGE

Arctic Circle

McKinley National Park

FAIRBANKS

Alaska RR

Yukon River

YUKON TERRITORY

ANCHORAGE

SEWARD

WHITTIER

Richardson Hwy

COPPER CENTER

TOK

Alaska Hwy

VALDEZ

DAWSON CITY

Columbia Glacier

BEAVER CREEK

Haines Hwy

WHITEHORSE

White Pass & Yukon RR

SKAGWAY

HAINES

JUNEAU

BRITISH COLUMBIA

SITKA

OLIKTOK

PETERSBURG

KETCHIKAN

CONTENTS

Foreword

Foreword

I was 70 when the first edition of this book was published. That was in 1985. It seemed reasonable to assume that my career in Alaska tourism was about complete. But in November 2004, surrounded by family and friends, I celebrated my 90th birthday. And as it turned out, the ensuing 20 years were as eventful as any period that came before. So in this third edition of Mr. Alaska, I have completed the story of my involvement in the Alaska travel industry.

I first saw Alaska as a pilot during World War II. Even during those bleak wartime years, I was enthralled by the beauty and grandeur. I had no idea then that — except for a 10-month tour of duty flying "the Hump" in China-Burma-India — the next 60 years of my life would involve Alaska and Alaska tourism.

In 1945 when I returned to Alaska to start a career as a bush pilot, tourism through the North Country was non-existent. There were no sightseeing services, no inter-city tourist coaches. Highways were dirt or gravel and filled with chuckholes and frost heaves. Hotels were "frontier." Their owners had no interest in the tourist trade.

Before the war, there had been overland tourist travel through Alaska and the Yukon. Ship passengers arriving in Skagway rode the White Pass & Yukon narrow-gauge railroad to Lake Bennett near the summit of White Pass where Klondike goldrushers had wintered in 1898. Some of these tourists continued on to Whitehorse and Dawson City.

Other passengers disembarked at Seward or Valdez and continued overland by rail or highway to Fairbanks, where a few venturesome souls boarded Yukon riverboats for the thousand-mile cruise through subarctic wilderness to Whitehorse and the railroad to Skagway. This enormous circle route was the pre-war "grand tour" of Alaska.

In those days there was no such thing as cruising in the modern sense of the word. Sea travel was limited to the cargo-passenger ships of the

Canadian railroads and the old Alaska Steamship Company.

And even this kind of tourist travel had ceased during the war. When I returned from Indochina, Alaska tourism existed in only one place; it was an idea inside my head. Everyone else in Alaska was caught up in a frenzy of post-war construction. They had no time for sightseers.

My first idea was to fly tourists from Fairbanks, 100 miles south of the Arctic Circle, to the old mining town of Nome on the Bering Sea and to the Eskimo village Kotzebue, where main street was a strip of gravel beach fronting the Arctic Ocean. Today, that same Nome-Kotzebue excursion is offered by every major tour company in Alaska.

Looking back as I begin my 90th year, that first idea seems modest, indeed, considering the extraordinary changes during the almost half-century since. Each of those changes has been the result of one more idea building on top of the others. Ideas can be powerful. They have a life of their own. Some let you down — and some others have totally unforeseen consequences. I'll tell you about those, too. But most were good ideas. They burned their way from inside my head out into the world. And most of them worked.

> Charles B. West
> April 1, 2005
> Issaquah, Washington

Chuck West, age 89, at his retreat
in Haines, Alaska in 2004.

PART I:

EARLY YEARS

Growing Up In Los Angeles

When I was fifteen I carried the *Hollywood Citizen News* on a daily delivery route. One afternoon when all the newsboys had gathered at the paper pickup point, a man approached and asked if any of us had an extra paper. One of the younger lads, a boy of ten or eleven, stepped forward with a paper, which the man took. He gave the boy a nickel and stood waiting for his change — at that time papers sold for three cents. The boy apologized for not having any pennies, and the man abruptly slapped him across the face with the folded newspaper, snarling, "All you damned kids are the same — trying to cheat me out of my two cents change."

When I protested that the man should not have done that, he drew back his fist and punched me in the mouth, splitting my lip. My response was pure outrage. I was only fifteen and not a large boy, but I was strong and well set up. I tackled the man, knocked him to the ground, and began pummeling him. A dozen punches were exchanged. The other boys were no help; they just stood by, shocked at seeing one of their own do battle with a grown man. The scuffle turned into an intense, bloody ripped-shirt brawl that moved from the street through an alley. The man, undoubtedly astonished at the sudden metamorphosis of a newsboy into a tiger, now tried to get away and took off running — followed by a strange procession of a half-dozen young boys led by a blood-spattered adolescent.

"Don't you dare follow me," he shouted over his shoulder as he ran out of the alley and down a boulevard.

"I'll follow you to hell until I find out where you live," I panted through battered lips. "You haven't seen the end of this."

The chase led to the man's apartment house and through the back door where the fight continued down the hallway, until neighbors in the apartment called the police. Our procession ended at the local station where the man accused me of assault and battery. Then my mother appeared, bringing with her character witnesses for her son. We — the newsboys and I — told our story in court and the judge sentenced the adult bully to three days in jail. We made the headlines: CORNER FRACAS — BOY AND MAN IN BLOODY BATTLE.

I wasn't a young tough, nor was I a belligerent kid trying to be a hero. I had responded to an unjust situation with a flare of temper. And I learned something. I learned that by standing up for the other boy and for myself, I gained the respect of the newsboys and I kept my own self-respect, as well. I realized then, and I believe now, that it is right to fight for what you believe in.

I was a competitor, even in grammar school where playground pastimes were marbles and "tops," and the shooter was entitled to keep any marbles or tops knocked out of the ring. On the playing fields of Hollywood we played "for keeps" — and I won a bag full of marbles and another of tops.

My family came to Los Angeles from Iowa in 1916. I was two; my sister, Mary Lou, three and one-half. Our father Louie LeFlore West, a traveling salesman for the Brown Shoe Company, was born in Holly Springs, Mississippi, descended from French traders and Indians — going back to the Choctaw chief Pushmataha (1765-1824). He had married Mary Mariah "Mae" Bigham, born of Scottish stock and reared in St. Joseph, Missouri. During World War I we moved to Los Angeles to be near my maternal grandparents. Soon after, the Brown Shoe Company turned entirely to war production, and my father enlisted as a first lieutenant in the infantry. Because of his age and family responsibilities, he was not asked to leave the country. He served in the Army on this side of the Atlantic.

We lived near my grandparents. My grandfather Bigham — a Civil War veteran, tall and erect, with goatee, moustache and a full head of hair — took delight in donning his Confederate uniform and marching in the Independence Day parades. We lost him in 1925 when I was eleven years old. Both grandparents were loving, stern, moral people who had worked hard all their lives and believed in hard work for everyone.

I remember appropriating my grandfather's knife from his bedroom table. I intended to carve a design in a backyard tree. After plunging the knife into the tree trunk, I broke the blade trying to pull it out. Not knowing what to do, I returned the knife to the bedside table and said nothing. Later my grandfather asked if it was I who had broken the knife. I said that it was. He asked why I had not told him about it. I said that I was afraid. He gave me a lecture on telling the truth. It was the kind of lecture one would expect from a loving, stern, moral, Scottish patriarch. And it made a powerful impression on me: "Never be afraid to tell the truth," he said. "When you make a mistake or do harm, own up to it. Never try to hide it. Never misrepresent or lie about something you've done." He bought me a knife of my own and taught me how to take care of it. Perhaps in memory of him, I carry a knife in my pocket to this day.

Around the house as a boy, I fed the chickens and mowed the lawn. When I was eight I started collecting newspapers, rags, and bottles and sold them to the man who drove through the neighborhood in a horse-drawn wagon, crying out, ''Rags, bottles, sacks.'' While pursuing this enterprise, I attracted a following of my peers whom I pressed into service as my helpers. At age ten I broke into the lawn care business, weeding lawns for neighbors, and collecting ten cents for each full bucket of weeds I dug.

My first regular job was delivering a shopping newspaper. At age twelve I was able to purchase a $1,000 life insurance policy. Even as a boy, I somehow always seemed to have walking-around money in my pocket. It was a good feeling; I never got over it. In high school I acted as class treasurer and managed the school candy stand, selling ice cream, soft drinks, and confections (some made by my mother). My bent was business.

I graduated from Hollywood High school just in time for the Great Depression — and I almost didn't graduate. In the summer of 1931 I had taken a job in a gasoline station. The job paid forty dollars a month, which helped support our family during the very bottom of the Depression. When it came time to return to high school in September, my father discouraged the idea — in those days a job was more precious than school. I was ready to go along with him but my mother prevailed. She wanted me to attend college some day, and for that I needed to finish high school.

During the twenties my father had been successful in the real estate business. However, many of his personal investments were paper equities and second mortgages, worthless when the nation plummeted into depression. We lost our home, our car — everything but our clothes and furniture. An aunt paid the first six-months' rent on the apartment we moved into. Our family was in difficult straits; and, humbling though it was, my father approached the Loyal Soap Company with the proposition that they consign him cases of soap which he proposed to sell by the bar, door to door. And that's what he did. He got a little wicker basket, filled it with soap, and set out each morning with his basket and a smile. I used to have tears in my eyes seeing my dad go out the door with his basket of soap. Some days he wouldn't sell a bar. But he kept at it, became a district manager for the soap company, and eventually a company officer. I believe that my father's perseverance in the face of adversity helped instill in me the will to keep up the struggle when things seemed impossible.

Luxuries in our home were minimal during those trying years. We depended upon one another for much of our entertainment. Though all the best things in life aren't free, my sister and I found that some of them were within reach. She taught me ballroom dancing. We read a lot, bringing home books from the local library.

Influenced by my mother, I did return to high school; and an experience during my senior year eventually led to a more substantial job than being a newsboy. As an officer of the senior class, I was invited to represent the school at a Rotary Club luncheon where I sat beside the manager of one of the local banks, a man named Harry Sherman. During our luncheon conversation, I explained to Sherman that I had passed the entrance examination to Stanford but would have to find a job and go to work before entering college. He invited me to call on him after I finished school. When that time came I went to the bank, diploma in hand, and was hired for the princely salary of $55 a month — upped to $65 when Franklin Roosevelt established a minimum wage.

I was a cocky young man, aggressive, sure of myself. Even in the conservative atmosphere of the bank my eagerness was considered an asset. I moved up from messenger boy to statement clerk and then to bookkeeper, where I met my nemesis in detail. They assigned me the task of recording each day's checks and balancing the books. My work was often inaccurate, causing me to stay after hours to find errors that I had made earlier in the day. Unable to force myself into the careful habits of a tabulating clerk, I decided to ask for a change of assignment. I was even ready to quit my job. I approached Harry Sherman and told him that I couldn't take the monotony; the job was dull and boring and gave me no opportunity to meet the public. Moreover, I admitted to performing poorly and without enthusiasm.

In response, Harry Sherman made me a surprising offer. ''Would you like to be a teller?'' he asked.

I said that I would — the job would mean working with the public.

Sherman then told me that the teller's job was open to me, but first I must prove myself by mastering the bookkeeping assignment. He made a little speech about not letting a job beat me and about the importance of my learning accuracy and curbing my impatience. He said, ''If you quit the bank, having failed in the work you were assigned, you will establish a bad precedent for yourself. Stay with this thing and beat it.'' He told me that if I would give him one month of error-free work, he would recommend me to the job of assistant teller.

That was good counsel; I took it to heart, slowed my pace, mastered the detail of my bookkeeping tasks and proved to Sherman — and to myself — that I could do the job. Good to his word, he put me into an assistant cashier's spot shortly thereafter. By the time I was twenty I was working in a teller's cage, meeting people, cashing checks, handling all that money.

When most of my high school classmates were entering college or struggling to find employment, I worked full time, earned a regular income and lived at home where my personal expenses were low. During years when most of Depression America struggled to survive, I had more discretionary income than I'd ever seen in my life. It wasn't long before I was driving around Hollywood Hills in my own sporty roadster — a used 1929 Model-A Ford, black with red wire wheels, two fender mount spares, and a chrome trunk rack — that I bought in 1934. I cut quite a swath through the younger set.

And the banking experience, brief as it turned out to be, gave me insights into the world of money. Before I was through I was to borrow a lot of it to finance ever-larger ventures in Alaska tourism.

I was never able to attend college full time, though I did go to night school, earning two and one-half years of college credits in business law, economics, banking, accounting and public speaking.

But about ten years earlier there had been another, totally unrelated experience that profoundly influenced the course of my life.

The Sky's The Limit

When I was eleven years old my Aunt Beulah took me and my sister Mary Lou on an airplane sightseeing ride. Snugged into the bucket seat of that tiny plane, I watched the pilot advance the throttle and for the first time in my life all my senses came alive at the same instant. The roar of the engine shut out everything else on earth. When I stuck my head around the windshield the prop blast whipped my hair, made my eyes water. Struts and guy wires hummed in the slipstream. Even the smells — hot oil, exhaust, fabric dope — were heady stuff for an eleven-year-old kid. The tiny plane surged, trembled, wanted to *go*, and the exhilaration I felt as we bounced down the runway into takeoff is beyond my powers to describe. I was *flying*, a part of the sky, looking *down* on earth. From that moment I knew that I must learn to fly or my life would not be complete. I waited nine years before I was both old enough and affluent enough to afford it.

By the time I was twenty my salary at the bank provided enough extra income to buy flying lessons. After eight hours of dual instruction, I soloed and then continued to build up flying time in Piper Cubs and Taylorcrafts at a cost of only four dollars an hour.

Two years later (in 1936), having decided once and for all that I was not cut out to be a banker, I sought a job in the airline industry. United Airlines' head man in Los Angeles was Homer Merchant. I picked up the phone and called him. When he asked what I could do — I told him; I had never been one to hide my light under a basket. I told him that because of my work at the bank I knew many local business people, understood where the money was, knew who was doing what, and when. I expressed faith and enthusiasm in the future of the airline industry. I told him I could bring him a lot of business. And I talked my way into an interview and a job, even though times were tough and the Depression was still going strong. Merchant offered me a position as salesman at a salary of $100 a month, $35 less than I made at the bank. I took it. I memorized United's schedules and prices, learned the business and sold a lot of airline space. One year later I was promoted to assistant manager of the Hollywood office, earning $165 a month.

Meanwhile I continued my hobby of private flying, joined a flying club, and logged many hours on the club's Interstate Cadet — my goal an instrument rating.

By 1940 I had become senior sales representative for United in the Hollywood district, and about this time United transferred me to New York. Unable to abide that frantic city, I accepted an offer from Western Airlines and moved back to Los Angeles. Among my assignments at Western was setting up package tours to national parks: Yellowstone, Glacier, Bryce Canyon, Zion, Death Valley, Jasper, Lethbridge, Banff and Lake Louise. I didn't know it at the time, but this experience was to prove invaluable a few years later in Alaska.

All the while I continued to fly, working toward a commercial ticket. As district sales manager for Western Airlines in Los Angeles, I was given authority to rent any private plane I liked to fly to speaking engagements with Chambers of Commerce and service clubs in California cities where I talked about the coming wonders of commercial aviation. By arriving in these towns as pilot of an airplane, I enhanced my credibility; I was an official of Western Airlines and a pilot as well — my word was gospel. I even became something of a radio personality. Radio station KFAC in Los Angeles suggested that I do a fifteen-minute weekly program, "Wings over the West," for Western Airlines. Audience reception was gratifying. I became the "voice of Western Airlines."

Then came the war. In June, 1940, I had gone to deliver airline tickets to a group of Frenchmen at the Hollywood Knickerbocker Hotel. Entering their suite, I was shocked to see these dignified men sitting about in their shirt sleeves, sobbing, tears streaming down their faces. Only minutes before, the men had learned that Paris had fallen to Hitler's Nazis (June 14, 1940). They were going home to a France occupied by the hated Boche.

That experience hit me hard. I became emotionally involved and decided to get into the fighting. I didn't meet the age and education requirements for the United States Army Air Corps, but Britain's Royal Air Force was less demanding. I hied myself down to an RAF recruiting office in Hollywood and volunteered.

Wiser heads prevailed and before I signed final papers with the RAF, Tom Wolfe, my boss at Western Airlines, talked me out of my impulsive gesture. He reminded me that our domestic airlines were essential to the war effort, and that I could make a more valuable contribution working in the airline industry than flying combat missions for the British.

Six months later, through a most unnerving incident, I learned of the United States' entry into World War II. On December 7, 1941, I was flying the Interstate Cadet over the San Fernando Valley. While practicing tailspins in an isolated chunk of air over Chatsworth Reservoir, I heard my call letters on the radio. A strained voice demanded that I return immediately to the Lockheed Termimal at Burbank and report to the operations office. My first thought was that I had violated some flying regulation. Had I spun down in front of other traffic? Or committed some other unforgiveble blunder? I cranked the plane into a sharp turn and headed for Burbank.

As I approached the field my ear phones crackled again: "Land ahead of the American Airlines DC-3," the control tower ordered, "and when you are on the ground, taxi your plane to the foot of the tower. There you will be met by a law officer." By this time I was thoroughly alarmed, convinced that I had committed a serious infraction and that the authorities were about to yank my license on the spot. After riding in a police car to police headquarters, I learned of the Japanese attack on Pearl Harbor and that all private aviation was grounded. They wanted to know who I was and why I was flying around up there.

Even many of the people who went through that period have difficulty recalling the consternation that seized the country following Pearl Harbor. The West Coast of America was virtually unprotected. No one had the slightest hint of what other plans the Japanese might have. It was easily conceivable that private aircraft might be used to bomb undefended plants such as Douglas, Lockheed and North American. The first thing the U.S. military did on that terrible December Sunday was pull every airplane out of the sky that could not be positively identifed, everything but scheduled airliners and military planes. I was grounded until some time later when regulations were relaxed.

About this time Marguerite Georgiana Lee came into my life. In the spring of 1942 I met a Scripps College girl on a blind date. Marguerite was different from other girls I had met. I thought I was pretty hot stuff — a Hollywood big shot. I had a good job with a major airline. I flew my own airplane and was a "radio personality" to boot. Marguerite was not in the least impressed — and that impressed me. Her family owned gold dredges in Nome, Alaska. She flew airplanes, herself; flying was not terribly adventuresome or glamorous to her. When I met her she was a student in chemistry and accounting at Scripps College in Claremont. We began to go out together and discovered that we had many interests in common. She was a solid, intelligent young woman with a good set of values, and I found her to be an immensely companionable girl. She was also a lovely girl, who had been awarded the title "Miss Alaska" in 1937 — an honor of such small importance to her that I never learned of it until long after we were married.

And I was eager to get married. She wanted to pursue a career in chemistry. In today's liberated world I'm not sure that I would have prevailed. But I convinced her. And we agreed to be married when she graduated from school. My first tie to Alaska was established.

Meanwhile, uncomfortable about hiding behind a draft exemption with a commercial airline, I moved on from my sales job at Western Airlines. In May of 1942 I volunteered to join the Civilian Pilot Training program and went to the CPT school at St. George, Utah, where I received special training in single-engined aircraft, acrobatics and night flying. But before signing my military commission as a flight instructor, I received a call from Fred Kelly, Western Airlines' chief pilot, who urged me to go back to work for Western flying military cargo to Alaska.

As a result of his call I joined the Air Transport Command and received training in multi-engine planes and instruments. Subsequently, I joined the Edmonton Division of WAL/ATC. Pilots rotated between Edmonton and Burbank, flying commercial airplanes for WAL and military craft for the ATC. Even our pay status reflected this arrangement. When I flew for the military out of Edmonton, I earned $440 a month military pay plus cost-of-living allowances; and when I flew out of Burbank, I earned $190 a month — straight wages.

Now that I was about to be married, I began to think more seriously about my finances. I had subscribed to a stock purchase plan while working for Security First National Bank, and later, at Western Airlines, I bought more stock the same way. These investments formed a small nest egg. I also had a little cash in the bank and my Plymouth coupe that I owned outright. I wasn't broke, but I wasn't flush either. I wanted to conserve our cash resources as much as possible and build up funds for our honeymoon and the start of our married life.

Airline pilots usually flew a certain number of hours or days each month and then were allowed time off. This interval gave me an opportunity to earn extra money. Answering an ad in the newspaper, I took a job delivering tons of new telephone books (and picking up old ones) door-to-door in a hilly section of Los Angeles. Having recently been the district sales manager for Western, I experienced a twinge of false pride as I lugged those telephone books through the Los Angeles foothills, hoping that I wouldn't be recognized by a former customer of the airline. Though I worried about my image, I made a lasting impression on my bride-to-be, who was pleased that her future husband wasn't above working up a sweat to provide for the household.

We were married April 25, 1943, at Toll Hall on the campus of Scripps College, just one day before Marguerite's graduation. After a short honeymoon at Warner Hot Springs in the San Diego Mountains, we made our home in the Griffith Park area of Los Angeles, but lived there only a short while before I transferred to Edmonton in central Alberta. We drove the

Plymouth coupe from California to Edmonton and discovered immediately that the housing situation was all but intolerable. Marguerite was resourceful and soon found a room for us in a private home.

When the woman who owned the home was called out of town for about six months, Marguerite took over her duties as landlady in exchange for our rent. The rooming house catered largely to oil company workers. Marguerite washed the bed linens and towels, down on her hands and knees, using an old-fashioned scrubbing board in the bathtub — adding more than her share to our cost-of-living expenses. We remained for about a year in that big old home, in a pleasant spot overlooking a golf course.

When I joined "Operation Sourdough," the Alaskan division of Western Airlines, I entered a completely new world of aviation. The Edmonton-Fairbanks-Nome run supplied America's bases in the far north and also connected with Soviet planes that picked up cargo in Alaska — everything from candy bars to aircraft engines — and flew it to their own bases across the Bering Sea in Siberia.

In his book *The Only Way to Fly*, Robert J. Serling wrote of that first winter's operation of Sourdough: "Temperatures sank to sixty-five below zero for weeks at a time. Rubber fittings crystallized to the point where the slightest touch would shatter them like fragile glass. Oil took on the consistency of thick mud, and grease simply froze in wheel bearings. Fuel hoses became so brittle they would snap in a modest wind. Altimeters, their air intakes often blocked by ice and heavy snow, could be a thousand feet off in either direction. Airports, at least in the early stages of the war, were nothing but dirt strips, and radio navigation aids were virtually nonexistent . . . Western never lost a plane or a man, and this perfect safety record could be classed as incredible, considering the technical handicaps under which it was achieved . . . by 1945, when Sourdough ended, WAL planes flying under the Air Transport Command flag had hauled more than twenty-two million tons, ranging from mattresses to Soviet gold being flown to the Denver mint."

I learned a lot about aviation during the twenty-one months I flew as pilot for the ATC. And I began to learn about Alaska. One more experience in my life anticipated my eventual career in the Alaska travel industry. First, though, another wartime adventure was to interrupt our lives. In May, 1944, I had an opportunity to join China National Aviation Corporation (CNAC) to fly supplies from India across the Himalayas — "The Hump" — into China. Because many of its early pilots and crews were drawn from Claire Chennault's Flying Tigers, the CNAC bore the unofficial title of "The Flying Tiger Line." The pay was great — up to $2,000 a month, and I would be close to the real action of the war, removed from the officiousness that permeated stateside military operations.

By this time, Marguerite and I had a baby daughter, CarraLee. Mother and daughter flew to Nome to join the Lee household there. I flew to New York — to Pan American World Airways which administered operations for the China National Aviation Corporation.

Flying "The Hump"

At Pan American headquarters in New York, I signed on, was briefed, and within a few days flew to Miami where I reported to Pan Am operations. In short order, I was put in command of a C-47 aircraft and assigned a co-pilot, navigator and radio operator — all army lieutenants bound for assignments overseas.

I was given a file of charts and maps and within a week took off in an olive-drab U.S. Army Air Force C-47, bound for Puerto Rico, Natal (Brazil), Ascension Island, Dakar, and across Africa's midsection to Aden in Saudi Arabia, and then to Karachi and Calcutta.

In India markings on the C-47 were changed from the USAAF to the insignia of the China National Aviation Corporation. Then I flew to the Upper Assam Valley for a week of training. The transition from Alaska to Indo-China came so swiftly that I had scarcely gotten my bearings before I was flying "The Hump" — in the middle of the action at last. I wore the uniform of the Chinese Air Force, my rank colonel, owing to an unhappy Japanese propensity for shooting captured prisoners whose rank was lower than colonel. The rank was a kind of macabre life insurance policy issued by Chiang Kai Shek and my employers at the CNAC. I thought it a nice gesture.

Before the Indo-China experience was finished, I was to fly one hundred fifty-three missions in and out of places like Dinjan in the Upper Assam Valley, and Kunming, Chungking, Chengtu, and Suifu (now called Yibin) on the Yangtze River. We flew in monsoons, sleet, snow, tricky winds — and over some of the most forbidding terrain on earth. Weather reports were primitive and undependable. Many times, loaded to the maximum, we took off on instruments from an airstrip in India to fly the entire route into China, without seeing the ground from takeoff to touchdown.

The skills of our Chinese co-pilots and radio operators were severely limited. Their main qualification was that they spoke marginal English. We were actually assigned a number of co-pilots who didn't know how to fly. American command pilots tuned the radios, handled gear and flaps — performed all functions of pilot, co-pilot, radio operator, flight engineer, navigator . . . instructor. A pilot had to be more than a "throttle-bender" to come away from "The Hump" alive. Skills in navigation and instrument flying had to be absolutely top drawer. My earlier experience flying in Alaska stood me in good stead. Before I left the Far East I became a night check pilot — more hazard, more money.

Skill wasn't everything. Luck counted too. Highly experienced pilots "bought the farm" because of conditions over which they had no control — tricks of weather, mechanical failures, not to mention Japanese fighters and fighter bombers. Sometimes we flew mercy missions to beleaguered Chinese troops cut off from their supply lines. On these flights we pinpointed troops on a map and flew over the location at tree top level, kicking stacks of rice bags, double sacked and eight high, out of the airplanes as we swooped over the drop zone. Flying low with engines throttled back, planes made easy targets for Japanese ground fire, usually small arms and machine guns. Hazards increased immensely because the total drop could not be made in one pass over the drop zone. Planes often took four or five passes before the entire load could be jettisoned. With each pass the likelihood of accurate ground fire increased.

I led one flight of five airplanes on a rice-dropping mission from which only two planes returned. The other three, hit by enemy fire, were forced into emergency landings or lost altogether. Returning from this mission, I thought I had escaped unscathed until the crew chief on the ground in India pointed to the tail of my airplane shot full of holes. I was to have received the Chinese medal "Order of the Flying Cloud" for that hazardous mission, but declined the honor. All missions were hazardous and crews killed during such Japanese attacks often didn't even receive decent burials.

Weather was as big a problem as the Japanese. Chinese meteorological people took a haphazard approach to reporting changes in wind direction and other conditions. One such instance nearly bought *me* the farm. I was beginning a letdown into Suifu. I had passed Tali Peak, which loomed up through the overcast, and throttled back to begin my descent at the standard rate of five hundred feet per minute. In the overcast I had no way of knowing that a strong headwind had reduced my speed in relation to the ground. I was dropping faster than I had calculated. When I popped out of the overcast I should have been near Suifu; but because of the headwind I was still way up the mountain, almost in the tree tops. I could actually see the rain glistening on the leaves of trees in front of me. Slamming everything to the fire wall — throttles, mixture, propeller pitch — I stood on the rudder pedal so hard that my leg quivered, dancing a jig. I know that I was yelling at the top of my lungs. My co-pilot just sat there, his eyes out on stalks. You're not supposed to wrench a big airplane around like that. As we climbed back into the overcast, still on instruments, I listened to the howls of protest from the airframe and prayed that the boys in Santa Monica knew what they were doing when they put that ship together. All I could think of was that I might be turning the wrong way, that we might be in a ravine with hills on both sides, or that the engine might quit just when we needed it the most. But we were lucky that day.

When we finally did land in Suifu, I walked into the operations shack and vented my feelings at the Chinese control operator who had talked to me on the radio — and not bothered to report the change in wind direction and velocity.

"So sorry, captain," was all he said. "So sorry. So sorry."

The Chinese word for "alert" is "jingbow." These alerts signaled the presence of Japanese aircraft. A "one-ball" jingbow (a red flare fired in the air) meant that enemy aircraft had been spotted; a "two-ball" meant they were headed for a CNAC target; a "three-ball" announced their arrival.

One black night — headed for Kunming fully loaded in terrible monsoon weather — I listened as my earphones announced a "two-ball" jingbow in Kunming. We were only one hundred miles out. "Two-ball" jingbows were often false alarms. I was low on fuel and out of patience. The rules said that I should have turned around and landed at the nearest safe airstrip. This would have meant returning to Burma to land in the mountains on an unlighted, unpaved strip whose hazards were probably no fewer than a quick fly-by of Japanese fighter bombers.

By the time that I was committed to landing at Kunming, the "two-ball" jingbow had become a "three-ball" affair. But even a full-fledged attack by the black-painted Japanese planes usually meant no more than a quick, low-level strafing run and dropping a couple of fragmentation bombs.

I was tired. I was almost home. And I was not pleased at all at the Japs for trying to mess up my airfield in the middle of the night when I was all but on final approach. I decided to bring the ship in, attack or no attack. If I encountered Japanese war planes . . . I'd think of something.

During a "three-ball" jingbow, the airfield always turned off all lights and assumed radio silence. In order not to be mistaken for the attackers and be shot down by the Chinese, I turned on all the lights on the aircraft — landing lights, cockpit and cabin lights, running lights. We looked like a juke box coming in for a landing. I also jazzed the throttles and fiddled with the prop-pitch controls, changing the rpms, making as much racket as possible. No Japanese pilot would do that. I hoped our ground forces would understand and not start shooting. My Chinese co-pilot and radio operator were in a wide-eyed panic.

Locating the airport was easy — just off the end of the lake — and even though the field lights had been turned off, my landing lights, reflected on the grass beside the runway, gave me my bearings. My procedural approach was strictly by the book: I turned the airplane into final approach, made a routine landing, taxied to the operations shack, found a place in line, parked the plane and shut down.

Lights were out in the air crew's hostel near the flight line, but once inside I could see a flickering light from the fire in the fireplace. I poured myself a cup of coffee and waited for the guys to start coming back from the bomb shelters. They greeted me with affection and warmth: "Are you the silly son-of-a-bitch who just landed that airplane?" I conceded that I was he. My commander was even *less* polite; he yelled at me. I could have been fired for breaking the rules but the plane was on the ground, the crew was safe, the cargo intact — and pilots were hard to come by. So he yelled at me some more and let it go at that.

I survived the China experience unscathed. Many of my fellow pilots were not so fortunate. More than once I was asked to look for wreckage of downed planes and signs of survivors. I found one wreck high on Tali Peak in Burma; there were no survivors. Another time, while flying to a rice-drop mission in China, we were attacked over Burma by Japanese fighters. I heard a "mayday" on my radio and looked around to see a parachute, then another, and then a burning airplane begin its long spiral into the Burmese jungle thousands of feet below. The Japanese fighter was apparently long gone. Throttling back, I circled the area, pinpointed the bail-out site on my navigational charts, and radioed the location to the nearest friendly Burmese base.

Only one of the two parachutists ever came out of that jungle. By the time they reached the ground, the two men were separated; each man was on his own. "Search and Rescue" could not locate them. The man who made it out managed to find a stream and follow it, living on leeches, frogs and other "guppy" fare. Friendly natives eventually took him to a military base — emaciated, suffering from malnutrition, insect bites, and every manner of discomfort. He had survived in that jungle nearly two months.

He could just as easily have been me.

The men who flew the Himalayan "Hump" regularly put their lives on the line, but it wasn't all hell fire and brimstone. Most of the flying officers held memberships in the British-American Club and Calcutta Swimming Club. There we found a haven in the midst of wartime deprivation — luxury in Calcutta, a dirty, noisy city whose population far outstripped its capacity for services. Within the Swimming Club compound were fine accommodations, a swimming pool, badminton courts, and recreation rooms where we could play cards, ping pong, or read. Weary pilots could also dine in fine restaurants and relax in comfortable lounges. There was even a race track.

Girls and every manner of vice were nearby, instantly available for those so inclined. I was dubbed "The Virgin" by my fellow pilots, but my lack of interest in boozing it up and patronizing the local girls was respected. I was no prig but I had no appetite for the excesses of liquor and whores in Calcutta.

The British-American Club became the site of an unusual celebration and reunion for me and one of my high school friends. Norman C. Geiger and I had gone to school together, played basketball and football, and enjoyed long bicycle jaunts to Santa Monica beach where we body surfed and eyed the girls. While I still worked for the bank, he and I drove across the country from Los Angeles to New York and back, just for a lark. Geiger worked in the publicity department of MGM studios in Hollywood. He was to have been best man at my wedding but the war interfered and we completely lost track of each other.

The scene shifts to the China-Burma theater. One day as I made a let down into the airport at Kunming, the voice of the tower operator through my earphones sounded somehow familiar. On the ground, I called Operations and asked who was the air controller on duty. "Corporal Geiger," I was told.

That was a happy chance meeting between two old friends, and not long after we learned that we both qualified for R & R — rest and relaxation. Geiger, being an enlisted man, was not supposed to leave his theater of operations. I managed to convince his commanding officer that the Corporal would be properly supervised if permitted to take leave in Calcutta.

Shortly before our takeoff from Kunming, Calcutta bound, we were asked to watch for a C-47 lost in northern Burma near Tali Peak. Norm, a trained observer, came forward and sat in the co-pilot's seat to help me look for the downed plane. Sure enough, we spotted it. The ship had crashed against a mountain. I reported the location by radio while doing a series of 90-degree banks in and out between the peaks. Now, a C-47 — in a sharp turn at high altitude — is not very spry. I could feel the plane lose lift, and so could Geiger. After a few such maneuvers he had had enough. "We've found the airplane," he yelled. "Now, for Christ's sake, let's get the hell out of here."

Once in Calcutta, we had a walloping good time at the British-American and Swimming Clubs. I managed to "promote" Corporal Geiger by outfitting him in a CNAC Colonel's uniform. The tall, good-looking Geiger cut quite a figure with the Red Cross nurses and other ladies he met. We chalked up enough experiences to make the Calcutta adventure an unforgettable furlough. Impersonating an officer was a court-martial offense, but during wartime — and in Calcutta — the pervasive who-gives-a-damn attitude made it the thing to do.

One of my most memorable flights came toward the end of my Indo-China experience. On New Year's Eve of 1945 when I reported to fly a C-47 to Dinjan, the Chinese operations man said to me, "Captain West, your crew not here."

"Where the hell are they?" I wanted to know.

"Party!" the Chinese man snickered. "They all at big party."

"When are they going to show up?"

"They not come at all, I think. All plenty drunk for New Year's."

Flight crews, wherever they are, celebrate New Year's Eve with vigor. I was a nondrinker and the only member of the assigned crew sober enough to make the flight. To turn down the flight simply because I had no copilot, engineer, navigator or radio operator would have caused me to lose face with the Chinese and income as well — night flights paid extra money. Also, the plane was needed in Dinjan at the other end of the line. There was no doubt that the flight would go as scheduled, whether I flew the airplane solo or the operations manager went down the list of pilots until he found one who was willing to take the trip, New Year's Eve or not.

The takeoff, though not a complicated procedure, kept me busy. Cowl flaps, wing flaps, landing gear, fuel mixture, throttles, prop pitch, trim tabs — all required my attention, as well as keeping track of RPMs and manifold pressure on both engines. But once off the ground and established in my climb, everything was routine. I trimmed out the plane, plowed through the cloud cover, and popped out on top at about 18,000 feet.

My God, it was awesome! The moon lighted tops of clouds just a few hundred feet beneath my wings. I envisioned the jagged mountain peaks hidden by layers of cottony fluff. For no reason that I could then — or can now — account for, I looked back into the empty cabin of the airplane; and the totality of my solitude came over me with the force of physical impact. As never before in my life — I was *alone*.

I had the whim to become a passenger. The whim became a compulsion. Setting the plane on automatic pilot and trimming her nose slightly downward, I unhooked my seat belt, removed my oxygen mask, got out of my seat and walked aft. The air was absolutely smooth. I sat down in one of the bucket seats that ran longitudinally along each side of the plane and gazed down at the panorama outside.

The engines purred. I was alone high above the Himalayas. In all my years I have never seen such an expanse of white clouds floating in the moonlight. I must have remained there in the after cabin fifteen minutes before reality intruded. Fifteen minutes at that altitude without oxygen was all that prudence would allow. I strolled back to the pilot's seat and clapped on my oxygen mask.

But the experience wasn't over. Donning radio earphones, I started to fiddle with the shortwave bands and — wonder of wonders — picked up San Francisco. The station was broadcasting music of one of the "big bands" of that era. There I was, nearly three and one-half miles above some of the most desolate terrain on earth, listening to great band music *live* from the ballroom of a luxury hotel in San Francisco. I could almost smell the perfume and hear ice tinkling in the glasses. I'll never forget it.

A few weeks later, returning from my last mission across The Hump, I received two important pieces of intelligence: I was eligible for an extended leave, and I was about to become a father again. I was ready for both. Having two children in diapers was a compelling reason to return to my family. Barbara Mae West was born in Nome shortly before I got back to the United States — in February of 1945.

While on R & R leave with my wife and in-laws in Nome, I talked with Sig Wien, one of the three Wien brothers of Wien Airlines in Alaska. The Wiens had obtained a contract with the U.S. Navy to establish airports that would facilitate development of oil fields in the far North. They were buying two twin-engined Boeing 247Ds — the first modern, all-metal, full-monocoque transports — but they had no pilots qualified to fly them. They needed multi-engine-trained pilots to carry out their Navy contract.

I was ready to stay home. Germany and Japan were on the run. With each new mission from India into China, I felt more and more like a fugitive from the Law of Averages. Sig Wien pulled strings through the Navy Department and secured my release from CNAC.

I stayed in Alaska to fly for the Wien brothers.

PART II:

GROWTH AND DEVELOPMENT OF ALASKA TOURISM

Bush Pilot

In 1945 I was a 31-year-old bush pilot flying for the Wien brothers — Sig, Fritz and Noel — of Wien Air, pioneers of Alaskan aviation. I flew into nearly all the tiny hamlets where during certain times of the year the bush plane was the only dependable means of transportation. My first passengers were emphatically not tourists. They were trappers, school teachers, miners, oil men, fur buyers, government workers, and ordinary citizens trying to get from one place to another across all-but-impassable Arctic wilderness.

The way people lived, their ethnic and cultural antecedents, were entirely new to a Depression kid from Los Angeles. Here was a land unlike any other on earth with its blending of primitive terrain, independent settlers, and still-unsettled frontier. I was enthralled by the majestic Alaskan landscape that unfolded beneath my wings — the forests, mountains, and limitless tundra prairies.

My introduction as an Alaska bush pilot had not been easy. I had done a lot of flying, I thought. With my Indo-China and previous Alaska experience behind me, I was prepared to take Alaska bush flying in stride, maybe even show the locals how it was done. I soon discovered that the locals already knew how it was done and that Alaskan bush flying was different from anything I had tried before. Putting down on a frozen lake or a mountain meadow was not the same as landing a multi-engine transport on a well-marked runway. I was to learn that Alaska pilots knew the Alaska bush as well as I knew Santa Monica Boulevard. And their casual attitude toward instruments and the other niceties of aviation protocol was utterly new to me.

Several personal experiences will acquaint you with the unique circumstances of flying in Alaska during those early days:

I was in Nome. Sig Wien had hired me solely on my credentials. To verify these he sent me to Nome station manager Dick Webb for the customary check ride. When I arrived at the field, Webb told me the line's senior bush pilot, Frank Whaley, was on holiday; and Whaley's understudy, Bill Peterson, didn't want the responsibility. There I was — wanting to prove my competence for the job, and no check pilot to go up with me.

Station manager Webb broke the impasse: "I'll go up," he volunteered.

"You a pilot?" I wanted to know.

He wasn't. But he assured me he could tell if I could fly an airplane. I had to accept that and he led me out in the snow to a Stinson Gull-Wing — on skis! I had never flown a ski plane in my life. Moreover, the plane was fully loaded for a flight to Kotzebue. All I could do was groan and ask questions of nonpilot Webb, my check-pilot commander. I suggested the plane be unloaded: I didn't know the Stinson's characteristics or how forgiving it might be. Taking off fully loaded could be chancy.

"Aw, you can do it," Webb assured me. "If we unload it now we'll just have to load it up again after the ride."

Only in the Alaskan bush did that kind of logic make sense. But there I was — in the Alaskan bush. So we climbed in and buckled up, and after I checked out the controls and instruments and figured out how to fire the engine, Webb called the Eskimo ground crew to pivot the plane on its skis. Pointed in the right direction, I began taxiing to the head of the runway where Webb instructed me to make a 90-degree turn and go through warmup procedure and mag check. I wanted to know what would keep us from running away (on skis) while the plane warmed up.

His advice was: "Just do it quick."

"Quick" turned out to be "instant," and there I was, turning into the runway on takeoff in a fully loaded, underwarmed plane — my first experience on skis, and the first of a variety of experiences that illustrated again and again the dashingly cavalier attitude of Alaskan bush pilots compared to the rest of the world.

We gained speed but not enough. With the snow-plowing, heavily loaded plane giving no sign that it would lift off, and the end of the runway coming up at an alarming rate, I chopped the throttle, kicked the rudder, and ground-looped untidily at the end of the airstrip.

Webb relented and summoned a ground crew to unload the Stinson into a truck. On our second try the plane lifted easily from the snow-covered runway. But my experience with nonpilot Webb had just begun: I had barely gotten the ship trimmed out and was starting to gain altitude when he wanted me to put the plane into a stall.

"At five hundred feet?" I protested. "Right over town?" And I may have added something to the effect of, "You're out of your mind."

Webb was unconcerned. "You've got to learn how this airplane behaves in a stall," he insisted.

I wondered if it had occurred to him that he was a passenger in the same plane that I was flying.

At a reasonable altitude and at an appropriate distance from town, I went through routine maneuvers — power-on stalls, a few tight turns. Back on the ground Webb allowed, ''I guess you can fly the airplane.''

But the day was not over. They wanted me to fly to Kotzebue. ''Where's that?'' I wanted to know. ''Up on the Arctic Ocean — two hundred miles.'' They had no map. I insisted on a map! They looked around and found a "Cat map,'' the kind Caterpillar tractor drivers use to find their way through the valleys. It had no contour lines to show elevations, no compass points, and blessed little other information to help an aerial navigator.

They reassured me. ''Ya see, right here.'' (pointing to the map) ''This is Asses' Ears Mountain — I'll mark that. First you go out here — ya see that valley? — you turn to the right through that valley, and when you get through you turn left by Asses' Ears Mountain, right about here.'' (another stab with the stub of a pencil) ''Keep going until you get to the Arctic Ocean — you'll know that right away because the ground, or really the sea ice, gets pretty flat although it's really bumpy — hummocky, you know? Then you just follow the shoreline which will bear toward the left, and you fly along there until you come to a long spit. Kotzebue is at the end of the spit. And you got it made.''

I had flown one hundred and fifty-three trips across the Himalayas, but I wasn't at all sure about Asses' Ears Mountain. ''How about radio contact?'' I wanted to know. And though their explanation of available radio navigation aids was even less reassuring than the map, I pointed the single-engine Stinson down the runway into a sunny, cold winter day.

Seated beside me in the small aircraft was a lady school teacher passenger. ''Isn't this a lovely day?'' she enthused. ''I've never been to Kotzebue.''

''Neither have I,'' I confessed, dividing my attention between the snowy terrain below and the rumpled map on my knees.

My confession didn't seem to bother her. Apparently she saw no problem in finding Kotzebue. Reassured, I flew on and soon located the valley they had marked on my map. I turned to the right through the valley and, sure enough, there was Asses' Ears Mountain. Gaining confidence, I turned left and kept going. There was the Arctic ocean — all bumpy and hummocky with sea ice. Then I just followed the shoreline which bore toward the left until I came to a long spit. And, sure enough, there was Kotzebue at the end of the spit. In no time at all I parked the Stinson beside Sig Wien's black-and-yellow Bellanca on the sea ice airstrip near the village. Kotzebue was, and still is, an Eskimo community on the Chukchi Sea, an arm of the Arctic Ocean.

My day was not over. Wien wanted me to follow his Bellanca 175 miles up the Arctic Coast to Point Hope where another school teacher awaited transportation back to Nome. Having survived both checkout pilot Webb and Asses' Ears Mountain in the same day, I was becoming more sure of myself. Still, I inquired about a more precise location for Point Hope.

"Don't you worry about it," Wien said. "Just follow me. About the only thing you'll have to watch out for are some chalk-white cliffs that stick up about twelve hundred feet or so. We'll fly out to sea a little ways and go around 'em. You just keep with me, and you'll be fine."

As it worked out, Wien's loaded Bellanca flew at a slower speed than my unburdened Stinson. I throttled down, playing horizontal see-saw with the other plane. This continued for some time until I became impatient. Visibility was good, the ground was in plain sight — why should I be leashed to the boss's wing tip? I switched on my radio, contacted Wien and advised, "I'm proceeding to Point Hope. See you there." I pushed the throttle to "cruise" and pulled ahead.

Mistake! I had no knowledge of the sudden whims of Alaskan weather or of the effect that a "white out" can have on a flyer's visibility — in a matter of minutes.

Fifteen minutes after I breezed past Wien, the coastline — my only reference point — disappeared. Ice fog! I didn't know the terrain, didn't know where the coastline curved, had not the slightest idea where to turn or let down. I asked myself — how does one distinguish a chalk-white cliff inside a chalk-white cloud?

To drop down through the white blanket of ice crystals without knowing what might lie below would have been madness. I had no choice but to fly the established compass heading and pray for a break in the overcast. None came. I had "flown out" my ETA (Estimated Time of Arrival). Fuel was low. Darkness was settling in. On the radio I announced to the Arctic vastness: "This is Chuck West in Stinson NC such and so, returning to Kotzebue."

Had I continued to fly on Sig Wien's wing tip as he had instructed me, all would have been peaches and cream. Sig knew the country, the weather, the landmarks. I didn't. I had flunked my first test with my new employer. Wien didn't appreciate the independence of his brash young pilot.

But I learned. Flying in Alaska one learns quickly and well, or a day comes when it's too late to learn anything at all. Wilderness flying in the Arctic is unforgiving of equipment failure or pilot blunder. Too often there is no second chance. Survival time for an injured, unprotected human in temperatures that drop to thirty, forty or fifty degrees below zero is measured in hours or minutes, not days. That was the essential difference between flying in Alaska and flying in Indo-China.

During that first year with Wien, I began to fly his twin-engine Boeing 247s on runs from Fairbanks to Point Barrow, Kotzebue, Nome, and St. Lawrence Island. We carried passengers and an unbelievable assortment of cargoes — bales of furs, Husky dogs and dog sleds, live reindeer, and all manner of provisions and equipment.

All the while I picked up great chunks of Alaskana that would later serve me well. My admiration for the determination and perseverance of the people grew.

Let me tell you about just two of those people. A bush plane had flown an elderly Scandinavian couple to Kotzebue from their cabin on the Kobuk River. I was to ferry them back to Fairbanks in one of the Boeing 247s. The wife had been a "mail-order" bride, coming to Alaska to make her life with a man named Swanson. They had lived off the land and the rivers, grown old, then frail, and finally almost helpless in the great wilderness.

A bush pilot had discovered their plight — alone without heat and food in the Arctic winter. The pilot had helped them into his plane on the snow-covered tundra near their cabin. Then the woman remembered she had forgotten her teeth and he slogged once again through the snow and plucked her teeth (and her dignity) from a nail over the wash basin. Taking off, he pointed his plane west toward Kotzebue Sound, following the Kobuk River, which flows out of the great barren humps of the Brooks Range north of the Arctic Circle. When he landed at Kotzebue we transferred his frail passengers to the twin-engine Boeing transport. With help the old man could walk. We moved the tiny woman by sled and I lifted her into the airplane. She couldn't have weighted more than seventy pounds. Both were in their nineties.

We wrapped them in blankets and I took off into a fantastic winter night, the Alaskan landscape lustrous in the moonlight. Turning the controls over to the co-pilot, I walked aft to the old couple and sat on the wing spar which ran transversely through the cabin of the 247. I took the tiny woman's hands in mine and asked how she was doing. She looked across to her husband and said, "Oh, Daddy. We're going to heaven. And he's the angel who is taking us there." She wore the sweetest expression I have ever seen. My God! That was heavy. I wasn't up to it and went back to the controls. In Fairbanks I went with them to the hospital. We were too late. In forty-eight hours both were gone — she first, then he, within hours of each other.

That same winter, I was flying from Fairbanks to Point Barrow when I learned that Barrow was socked in. Ice fog had moved off the Arctic Ocean and built up against the Brooks Range, a common weather pattern in that part of the world. We got as far as Umiat, a tiny community on the Colville River, where we had to put down. Then fog moved into Umiat. We were stuck.

We arrived there December 29 and were still there New Year's Eve. Each morning I went outside and eyed the weather. Stinko! Each morning I went to the field, heated and started the Boeing's engines and checked the weather at Barrow by radio, hoping it would have improved enough to take off. No luck.

Sig Wien was there. With his easy-going temperament, he could lie on his bunk for a month waiting for the weather to break. Not me. On New Year's Eve I told him I was leaving: "I'm getting out of here." Wien lectured me about my impatience but left the decision to me.

New Year's morning a three-hundred foot overcast shrouded Umiat. At Barrow weather was also "marginal." I had decided to take off, climb out of the overcast, and — once on top, estimated to be two thousand feet — check the weather by radio and make the decision whether to head for Barrow or return to Fairbanks. On board were two Navy personnel and my co-pilot, a man named Dolph Schoenberger. We carried enough gas to fly to Barrow, with Bettles on the south slope of the Brooks Range as an alternate.

When we broke out of the overcast, we learned that weather in Barrow was still "marginal." Sitting up there in the Arctic twilight, looking down on the clouds, I conferred with Dolph. We decided to try for Barrow and I pointed the Boeing northwest.

An hour later I began to let down through the overcast. When the altimeter registered three hundred feet, we were still in the clouds. I climbed and circled, and told Dolph we would try once more — at two hundred feet. This time we glimpsed the ground through the fog, but not the runway. Circling again, we came in at one hundred feet; and faintly through the mist, I saw the radio range tower go by our left wing as we passed to the right of the field. With quarter-mile visibility and a one hundred foot ceiling, we circled and landed on Barrow's steel mat runway.

I would never have survived had I continued my career as a bush pilot in Alaska. I was too impatient and sooner or later my impatience would have killed me — and perhaps others along with me. I would have had to change my entire outlook to survive. I was a skilled pilot but I couldn't lie on my bunk for a month waiting for the weather to change.

In the winter of 1946 I barely squeaked through on a flight with the Boeing 247D. Two competing fur buyers, one known as Gus the Greek, the other as Johnny Muskrat, were anxious to fly from Nome to St. Lawrence Island in the Bering Sea south of the Chukchi Peninsula (Siberia). They hated each other, and each wanted to be the first to charter a flight to buy those furs. On this particular day Gus the Greek had reserved a charter, and I was "up" for the flight. Weather at St. Lawrence was marginal, a 200-foot ceiling and tail winds going out. The primitive weather station at St. Lawrence was little help to pilots, and the Russians were no help at all. Weather in that part of the world moves from west to east; pilots could never tell what might be descending on them from Siberia. We were very much on our own.

I conferred with my co-pilot and we decided to take the risk. At "first light," about ten o'clock in the morning in the short winter days of the Arctic, the Boeing lifted off Nome runway: our only passenger, Gus the Greek. At 4,500 feet we climbed out on top of the clouds. We carried four hours of fuel to take us four hundred plus miles round trip — an hour and one-half out to St. Lawrence Island, an hour and one-half back, and an hour reserve.

The only ground-based navigational aid was a weak directional finder station at St. Lawrence Island. About an hour out of Nome, we lost its signal and I realized that we had been drifting north. Correcting the course, I picked up the station and once again we beamed in on our destination. Twenty minutes later I estimated we should be getting close and began to let down through the cloud cover, and just at that moment the St. Lawrence radio station went off the air!

I had two options: I could continue my let down and search for the island, or I could return to Nome. We were somewhere in the middle of the Bering Sea with no navigational aids and no way of knowing our location. I decided to give St. Lawrence one last try and continued my let down, making a twenty degree turn to the right. At about eight hundred feet, we dropped out of the clouds and I began a left turn because that was where the last signal had come from. Then I glanced to the right. And saw land? If St. Lawrence was to the left, what was the land mass on my right? Suddenly I knew. I had been blown more than fifty miles off course in a northwesterly direction — and was looking straight at *Siberia*.

Two important questions: How strong was the headwind going back? Did we have enough fuel to reach Nome? I put the Boeing into a climb, got back on top of the clouds again, took a compass reading and headed for home. Gus the Greek was having conniptions. All he could think of was that his arch rival, Johnny Muskrat, would beat him to those St. Lawrence furs. "Hey," he yelled, "We gotta land. We gotta land."

"Sit down, Gus," I told him. "I'm going to fix it so we don't have to swim home."

If I veered to the right of our course, the radio signal from Nome was a Morse Code "A"; if I veered to the left, it was a Morse "N." After we had flown for about an hour, Nome gave me a position fix that was not in the least reassuring. With the fuel that remained in the tanks and with the distance that remained to fly, combined with the head wind, I was sure that we would not be putting down on anything as civilized as a runway.

I radioed Nome and told them to look for us on the sea ice about forty miles out. Not long after, a Coast Guard plane showed up and hung on our wing. We talked back and forth between the two planes. To stretch the fuel as far as possible, I "leaned out" the carburetor mixture and backed off on the throttles. Then I dropped down to about one thousand feet off the ice; if we were forced to land, the Coast Guard would know where we were and could direct help without delay. Except for Gus, the co-pilot and myself, the plane was empty.

We had been in the air well over four hours when I saw — now showing on the horizon — the breakwater that protected the runway. I couldn't believe it. And rest assured, I didn't circle the field. I went straight in and pulled back on the power as soon as we cleared the breakwater. We touched down. We were on the runway.

And the *instant* the tail wheel touched ground both engines quit. So little fuel remained in the tanks that when the attitude of the plane changed, fuel sloshed to the backs of the tanks where the pumps couldn't pick it up. The ground crew had to tow the plane off the runway to the hangar. That was as close as I ever want to cut it.

An Idea

All the while during those bush pilot days — during the cargo flights, the passenger flights, the rescue flights — my enchantment with the land and the people grew. And an idea grew along with it. If the land enchanted *me*, why not others? We could draw tourist travelers — just sightseers — from Fairbanks, take them round trip to Nome and Kotzebue, walk them through an Eskimo village, show them houses built on stilts, recount Nome's gold rush history, return to Fairbanks past the icy slopes of Mt. McKinley. In a single busy day we could give travelers the flavor of this great land and a glimpse of the people who inhabited it. Alaska is immense: there were sourdoughs who had lived their entire lives in the interior and never seen an Eskimo.

In Fairbanks I had become active in the Junior Chamber of Commerce. There, and with friends — with everyone I met — my dreams of Alaska tourism bubbled over, wouldn't be contained. Almost everyone shared my enthusiasm. Everyone, that is, except Sig Wien.

Wien talked in a slow John Wayne kind of drawl. In response to my carefully planned proposal, he replied. "Well, Chuck, you know, we are flying these airplanes to Nome and to Kotzebue and to the villages, and we publish a schedule and we establish a fare. If people want to fly with us as tourists, we'll carry them like anyone else. We've never denied people passage on our airplanes."

If Wien's slow drawl was John Wayne, my rapid-fire staccato was James Cagney. We played a little scene:

WEST: "I'm talking about *promoting* the idea, letting people know how much there is to see out there."

WIEN: "I don't think we're ready for anything like that just now."

WEST: "People who've never been to the Arctic can't know about the excitement out there unless we advertise it — brochures, pamphlets. Get the word out.''

WIEN: (*very* slowly, deliberately): ''I don't think we should spend our time and our money trying to develop more business when we're already busy with what we're doing.''

Hearing nothing but negatives, I was forced, for the moment, to give up on Wien. But I wasn't giving up on the idea.

All of the seemingly miscellaneous pieces of my background began to fit together. My experience with package tours at Western Airlines kept prodding me. Fairbanks radio station KFAR put me on the air with a weekly ''Wings Over the North'' broadcast, patterned after my earlier show in Los Angeles.

Station manager Al Bramstedt listened to my idea about tourist flights to the Arctic and accepted my invitation to accompany me on a trial run. One clear day we took off for Barrow, and even though the flight had a few rough edges — we encountered all kinds of weather, nearly ran out of fuel, made two unscheduled instrument let downs — we nonetheless saw an enormous expanse of Alaska. Bramstedt returned from the flight enthusiastic about my plan, a booster of air tours to the Arctic. He gave me permission to mention Wien Airlines on the radio show.

He also asked the station for a budget to develop further promotion — while I went back to Wien, citing the radio station's support as evidence of public acceptance. Once again I pleaded my cause: would he schedule a trial one-day excursion flight, not for fur buyers, gold miners or oil prospectors, but for sightseers — a flight geared solely to the needs of the aerial tourist. Well, he would have to think about it. After powwowing with his two brothers and his financial man, he gave the plan an OK, though grudgingly. In today's parlance, all systems were ''go.''

I believe that if the Olympic Games had an event that measured enthusiasm, I'd take the Gold. It's not an attribute that I control. It's me. As much as anything else my capacity for enthusiasm has been responsible for my successes — as well as my setbacks when misdirected.

Now it was up to me; I had a sales job to do — and nothing sells like enthusiasm. The excursion would be a fourteen-hour, round-trip flight from Fairbanks to Kotzebue, Nome, and the Diomede Islands. The cost was a modest $75. We needed ten people (passenger capacity of the Boeing 247). I talked it up to anyone who would listen, broadcast it over the weekly radio show; and the flight filled up — ZAP! I learned that it wasn't at all difficult to find ten Fairbanks locals who wanted to take a Saturday off and explore the Alaskan ''outback.''

The reader should understand that I've never been one to hide my light under a basket or take a back seat. I was in my glory. The package was *mine*. I conceived it, sold it first to Wien, then to the passengers, took the bookings, flew the airplane, and provided a running commentary while in flight. If the idea was a flop there was certainly no one but myself to blame. On the other hand, if it was received favorably . . .

Knowing that the day would be long and that passengers would be hungry, I arranged with Archie Ferguson, owner of the general store and restaurant in Kotzebue, to serve a hot meal. Archie's mistress, an outgoing lady of generous proportions, pitched in with gusto and prepared a feast for passengers and crew.

Our small band walked through the village and down the beach. We saw fish drying on the racks, admired sled dogs tied to their primitive kennels, studied a Beluga whale dragged up on shore. For visitors from interior Alaska who had never seen how the coastal peoples lived, it was a fascinating experience.

We explored Nome the same way. I talked about the history of Nome and explained how in 1898 gold was discovered in nearby streams, and in Nome's beaches a year later. Turn-of-the-century miners washed millions from the most valuable beachfront property on earth. News of the gold rush soon reached Seattle and by 1900 Nome's population exploded to thirty thousand. In just two months Nome's beaches yielded more than $1 million in gold — when the value of the precious metal was fixed at eighteen dollars an ounce. A nugget that weighed nearly twelve and one-half pounds, one of the largest found in Alaska, was taken near Nome. At first, gold was taken by shovel, pickax, wheelbarrow, "rocker" or primitive sluice box. As years went by, more sophisticated machinery took over. Huge dredges moved in; their tailing piles, overgrown by willow, are still seen today in the flats behind town.

Like Kotzebue, Nome fringes the ocean beach. Huge boulders are piled high to protect the town from winter storms that blow in from the Bering Sea. Much of the town is built on permanently frozen subsoil (permafrost), which shifts around, forming an unstable foundation for buildings that are canted this way and that because of their uncertain footing. Walking down the wooden sidewalks of Nome's Front Street suggests walking through a Hollywood Western movie set after the buildings have been on an all-night spree.

We also flew out to the International Date Line between the Diomede Islands a few miles west of the tip of Seward Peninsula. Big Diomede is in Russia, Little Diomede in the United States. Such flights were discontinued in 1949 at the request of the U.S. State Department — the Russians considered them a violation of their "territorial integrity."

On the flight home, I turned the controls over to the co-pilot and went back to the cabin to point out the landmarks that slipped by under the wings. I was buoyant with success. Weather had cooperated. We had made no unscheduled instrument let downs. Travelers returned home from an exciting and rewarding trip, singing the praises of the inventive young pilot and budding entrepreneur who had dreamed up this marvelous diversion. It was an eye opener for them — and an eye opener for the budding young entrepreneur: if ten could be so easily recruited for an Arctic tour, thousands more must be waiting to be seduced by the Alaskan wilderness.

I went back to Wien; we played another scene, this time in the hangar.

WEST (rapid fire): "I believe in the future of these excursions. I'm ready to get out of the cockpit and spend full time promoting them."

WIEN (very slowly, deliberately): "I'm sorry, I'm just not willing to go out on a limb for your scheme."

WEST: "I'll even take a cut in salary to continue what I've started."

WIEN: "We've never done anything like this before, and just because it worked once is no sign it will work again."

WEST: "I'm making eight hundred a month now. Cut it to six hundred and give me a chance to prove the idea."

WIEN: "Six hundred dollars a month? That's as much as my brother Fritz is making."

WEST (becoming irritated): "What does that have to do with it? If I can't return your investment many times over, I'll forget the idea and go back to flying full time."

WIEN: "I don't like taking part in a gamble. But OK, you can try it."

West left the hangar — walking on air — blissfully unconcerned that he lacked a sales department, an ad department, or a customer relations staff.

Initially, the promotion I planned took three forms: weekly pitches advertising the flights on "Wings Over the North" broadcasts, word-of-mouth promotion with the Junior Chamber of Commerce, and printed notices posted wherever they might do some good. It didn't hurt, at all, that during the summer of 1946 Eielson and Ladd Air Force Bases boomed with military construction. Fairbanks overflowed with thousands of construction workers from "Outside" who were paid by cost-plus contracts and had money and time to spare — as well as an eager curiosity about Alaska. These cheechakos were a great source of business. (One of my prime spots for posting tour notices was in construction site latrines — where workers might have a few extra minutes to read.)

The Arctic Coast tours were outrageously successful. Wien's airplanes filled with tourists. He couldn't carry them all. Many went away disappointed because we didn't have space on the day they wanted to go. Many others returned for a second trip. I had discovered a lucrative business — filling the demand for "pocket-sized" package excursions into the Alaskan bush.

I went back to Sig Wien, feeling that I had proved my point. The airline had earned handsome revenues and enjoyed other promotional benefits. Now we should expand the idea; I asked for an advertising budget, a secretary, and a travel allowance to go "Outside" and promote in the South 48. I was convinced that, given half a chance and a bit of selling, the idea could become a real money maker.

I was stunned by Wien's response: "We need you back in the air as a pilot, Chuck. We've got a lot of business contracted for the winter. Maybe we can talk about this tour thing again next summer."

And that was the end of it. I was crushed — and angry, erupting with stifled enthusiasm. But I got back into the cockpit and flew when and where I was told. Soon though I realized that my temperament (and temper) would never mesh with the Wiens' stand-pat philosophy. They preferred the status quo to growing pains. If I wanted to grow I'd have to do it myself. That would mean leaving the airline and starting my own business.

That was autumn of 1946. I talked to my wife, Marguerite. We lived in a log cabin near Fairbanks where we enjoyed two luxuries: electricity and running water — when the water didn't freeze. We now had three children: CarraLee, Barbara, and four-month-old Charles (born in July of the preceding summer, 1946). Winter was coming on, a tough time (one hundred miles south of the Arctic Circle) to make hard decisions. We put our heads together and concluded we would be happy only when we controlled our own destinies. The pressing question was whether to move now or later. Should I put aside my dreams for establishing my own travel business and continue as a Wien pilot for another season? Or should I break cleanly and immediately with Wien and begin plans now for next spring?

I reminded Marguerite that Northwest Airlines had begun flights into Anchorage. Some of those passengers would want to see more of Alaska. We could arrange package tours to bring them to Fairbanks and then take them out to Nome and Kotzebue. Northwest would need representation in Alaska — there wasn't a travel agent in the entire Territory. I could start a tour program and a travel agency at the same time.

Marguerite agreed: "Let's do it. You can always go back to flying if things don't work out."

Still the cocky, self-assured promoter, I went to Sig Wien and announced my plans, boasting that I would make more money for the airline than I would have produced had I remained on its payroll. Brash to the end, I held on to my confidence even when members of the company board of directors — Sig, Fritz, and Noel Wien, and George Rayburn — individually came to our cabin urging me not to leave their employ.

I told them, "It's now or never. If I'm going to make this thing come true, I've got to be free to do it my way."

I had stepped into a fantasy world. What I swore I would do had never been tried before. The idea was as untested as I was; and I had yet to prove myself — to my former employers, to the industry, to my family.

I quit Wien Airlines in November of 1946 and I looked forward to a hard Alaskan winter, seduced by a vision — my next paycheck as nebulous as the Northern Lights.

A Cold Winter In Fairbanks

In November of 1946 I applied to the Air Traffic Conference for appointments to operate a travel agency. Marguerite and I had selected the name "Arctic Alaska Travel Service." I now had a name and a hip pocket to operate out of. But how would a neophyte travel agent find customers in the dead of winter — in Fairbanks? My goal was to build a package tour business, but such tours had little potential for income until late spring and summer. How were we to make it through the winter without dipping into savings? We would need those savings to promote our tours when the travel season started next spring.

Several small feeder airlines fanned out from Fairbanks, serving an enormous territory and a host of tiny communities. In most parts of the world, even the larger of those communities — McGrath, Nome, Barrow, Fort Yukon — would have been mere villages. Scattered across the vast spaces between these "centers" were — are — hundreds of tiny habitations — mining camps, missions, trading posts, riverboat stops, Eskimo and Indian villages — pinpoints with names like Tanana, Holy Cross, Unalakleet, Eagle, Crooked Creek. And no matter how remote the community or how rugged its setting, there was always a space nearby for a primitive airstrip. Bush planes put down on mountain meadows, gravel bars, Arctic sea ice, frozen lakes or gold dredge tailing piles leveled into runways. From far-flung outposts throughout Alaska, travelers funneled into Fairbanks and Anchorage where many connected with flights "Outside." Pan American flew Fairbanks-Seattle; Northwest Airlines, Anchorage-Seattle.

My experience working for Western and United in Los Angeles had given me an understanding of airline sales operations. I believed that I could increase Northwest Airlines' business from Anchorage to the South 48 by acting as the airline's agent in Fairbanks. I would sell tickets to passengers who arrived in Fairbanks from smaller communities and who needed a connection to Seattle and other points, and I would route these passengers via Northwest Airlines flights from Anchorage. I went to Northwest's district manager in Anchorage, Bob Wright, and proposed that I be his agent in Alaska.

Wright (later Northwest's senior vice president in charge of marketing) agreed to my proposal: "You just sell the tickets and we'll pay a commission. He volunteered to help me obtain the Air Traffic Conference (ATC) appointment required to qualify for these commissions. Then I learned the appointment ritual would take time: I needed a bond, a location, and a certain level of experience. I had hoped to be ready for the Christmas season when many Alaskans fly south. As it turned out, the appointment did not come through until February.

Meanwhile, I faced bleak prospects while I waited for the summer season. But I had to begin somewhere. The first step was to set up a base of operations. Any old hole-in-the-wall would do, and that's what I settled for — an unfurnished, uninsulated space in a First Avenue warehouse owned by the Wilbur Plumbing and Heating Company. It had little to recommend it except low rent of $100 a month and a kerosene stove.

With no furniture and no budget to buy any, I did what any imaginative pauper would have done: I went to the Navy dump, found a desk (two legs missing), carted it off, cleaned it up, fashioned replacement legs. From home I commandeered an old kitchen chair and Marguerite's portable typewriter. A filing basket, new, put a final flourish on the office appointments, and for $25 a sign painter lettered "Arctic Alaska Travel Service" on a large board which I hammered into place on the front of the building.

I had "hung up my shingle." And though I had no appointments and no income in sight, I was in business.

I also had a family to support. What to do?

American Airlines had begun flying cargo into Fairbanks. They would need ground services and personnel. I contacted American's James Wooten (later to become Alaska Airlines' president), told him my background and suggested that I be American's ground crew and "go-fer" in Fairbanks. For $20 per plane arrival, I would see that gas trucks fueled the airplanes, that the pilots got hot meals, that wheels were chocked and gust locks placed and removed, and that some responsible person would help with flight plans and coordinate ground activities for American's flights.

I got the assignment — and was that a howl! Some mornings I was at the field by 4:00 a.m. to stand in forty-below weather in the prop wash under the engine cowling of those DC-4s, hand energizing the starters that helped the engines fire. Even though I wore a heavy hooded parka and stood with my back to the propeller blasts, I've never felt such piercing cold. Seldom would an engine start on the first try, and with each successive try the propeller sent back increasingly stronger blasts of piercing cold air. Sometimes the force of the blast was so strong that it sent me slipping and sliding across the ice — tough work, but I was making enough money to survive. And in a way I kind of enjoyed it.

I also started another enterprise, a partnership with Herb Pickering, who owned a grocery store. At that time a maritime strike had interrupted the flow of ship cargo to Alaska, forcing many businesses in Fairbanks to ship goods by air, an expensive alternative to the usual steamship-rail cargo route. Any number of small, nonscheduled (non-sched) charter airlines had begun flying to Alaska during the shipping shortage. Pickering and I formed Alaska Air Cargo Consolidators, taking orders from many local businesses and "consolidating" their shipments on planes that we chartered from Boeing Field in Seattle. Our service enabled local firms to pool their shipping needs and reduce costs accordingly.

Meanwhile, I couldn't lose sight of my principal objective, the Alaska package tour business. I decided to attend the first postwar American Society of Travel Agents (ASTA) conference to be held in Del Mar, California. I wanted to talk to travel agents about my plans and arranged with a friend to take over the airport ground services job, while I bummed a free ride south on one of the non-sched airlines.

During my two-week absence Marguerite endured one of the coldest Januarys in Fairbanks' history: the mercury dropped to 68 degrees below zero. Sewers and water lines froze. She had three babies to care for. The heating system in our log cabin was a furnace, a wood pile — and an ax. Before leaving for Del Mar, I reminded her that the ax was sharp and reassured her: "You're going to be fine." She remembered that reassurance every time she left the comparative warmth of the cabin to chop wood in the Arctic blasts of that Fairbanks winter, all the while thinking of me in Southern California. But our marriage survived that January. And it has endured and grown during the four decades since.

Agents who attended the ASTA convention in Del Mar were enthusiastic about my plans to develop Alaska tour packages. They told me to go back and prepare a folder describing the itineraries, prices, departure dates, and other pertinent information. I spent a profitable two weeks in Del Mar testing the waters, making contacts and building plans for tourism in the Arctic.

When my appointment as an authorized Northwest Airlines agent came through in February (1947), I gave up the ground crew operation, abandoned the air freight/air forwarding partnership with Pickering, and went into the travel business full time.

Then it was almost prophetic how seemingly unrelated pieces of my background and experience began to mesh. While working at the airport, I had watched the cargo planes fly into Fairbanks loaded to capacity and return to the South 48 empty. The non-sched airlines (Northern, Golden

North, Northern Consolidated, Sourdough Air Transport, General Air Cargo, and others) did a land-office business — *one way only.*

I had an idea that would fix that. Most of the planes were converted military transports with bucket seats, hard and cold — but capable of hauling passengers. I went to the airlines, ready to bet my last dollar that I could sell southbound tickets for $100 a pop, $50 less than Pan American got for regular passenger flights. I proposed that I fill their airplanes on their return flights southbound. My commission would be $20 per seat sold. "You get $80 and I get $20," I told them. "And I'll escort your passengers to the airport and put them on your airplanes."

I began selling tickets on the non-sched airlines, and the idea was an instant success. Planes filled with construction workers and others who were looking for an inexpensive ride to the South 48. During the first six months of this endeavor, spring and summer of 1947, I earned $23,000 — not bad money in those days. As with every success, it soon had its imitators; I was not the only one in Fairbanks selling seats on non-sched airplanes. Every bootblack in town, it seemed, got in on the act — also bartenders, barbers, and hangers-on.

Predictably, the scheduled airlines began to cut prices when they saw their revenues drop. At first they matched the $100 non-sched fare. Then a price war began — $90, $80, $70, even $60 would get you a ticket to Seattle. It didn't take me long to realize that the big commercial carriers would be the eventual winners in this war.

But we had survived the winter and I was on my way.

"Arctic Alaska Tours" Takes Off

My original plan had been to use scheduled Wien aircraft to carry sightseeing tourists from Fairbanks to Nome and Kotzebue. Now, the same cargo planes that had formed the basis for my non-sched passenger business to Seattle also provided the service I needed for air tours to the Arctic. After bringing in their loads of freight, the planes usually remained in Fairbanks a day or two before returning to the South 48. During these layovers I was able to charter them at low cost for sightseeing excursions into the Arctic. And by doubling as navigator/co-pilot for the aircraft and as sightseeing guide for the tour, I saved even more on costs. Those were busy trips — I piloted the plane, provided commentary as we flew over the Alaskan wilderness, escorted people on the ground, and made sure lunch was prepared and that all other arrangements were in order.

Early in that 1947 season, I hired two young women part time to help as guides, Ginny Hill and Celia Hunter, both former WASPs (Women's Air Force Service Pilots). The two later established Camp Denali, the wilderness lodge near Mt. McKinley, and were successful in operating that facility for a number of years before selling to Wally Cole and his wife, who had been with McKinley Park Hotel.

Business for our Arctic tours increased to about one flight a week, drawing customers who were still primarily local — the construction workers who filled Fairbanks to overflowing. One of my main marketing "points" was still construction site latrines, where handbills advertising the tours were posted.

As the season developed, the Arctic excursions evolved into overnight, two-day packages. We spent the night at Archie Ferguson's store-restaurant-hotel in Kotzebue and used the extra day to visit nearby native villages where I hired Eskimo dancers and blanket tossers. The Eskimos are highly intelligent, talented people who through countless centuries have evolved the remarkable skills needed to survive in the Arctic. But they were shy and timid about performing their dances for strangers. To encourage them during their initial performance and be sure that they would show up, I announced to the village elders that I would bring an ice cream cone for everyone who came to the dance, to be performed on the Arctic beach. From Fairbanks I flew in a container of ice cream in a freezer pouch and a case of cones. After the dance the Eskimos lined up along the beach, at least one hundred and fifty of them, while I stood there scooping out ice cream cones for old people, young people, kids — they all got ice cream cones.

We also rigged a skin boat (umiak) with an outboard motor and took visitors across Kotzebue Sound to a village on the northwest coast where we observed native crafts people carve ivory and weave baskets. The more adventurous tourists sampled muktuk, an Eskimo delicacy made from the outer, corky layers of epidermis of bowhead and beluga whale. Eaten fresh, frozen, cooked or pickled, muktuk has been described as tasting like "pieces of innertube soaked in codliver oil." We also sampled more conventional fare: salmon, sheefish (a kind of pink-fleshed Arctic char), and reindeer steaks with blueberries picked wild and prepared any number of ways.

That cross-sound excursion in the skin-covered umiak would be completely out of the question today. The craft carried no life jackets or any other kind of flotation gear, and for this and other reasons would never have gotten past modern Coast Guard regulations. Nor did I carry any insurance.

At Nome we walked the beach line, recreated Nome's gold rush history, and explained the workings of an old gold dredge. Hungry travelers were taken to the North Pole Bakery Polar Room for a meal of reindeer stew and fresh blueberry pie.

We had few dissatisfied customers — most of them saw what they came to see and experienced a kind of hands-on contact with the magic of the Far North.

Back at the First Avenue warehouse office in Fairbanks, our days were filled with activity as we booked tours, sold air transportation south, and served as a travel agency for those Fairbanks residents who needed travel arrangements to other parts of the world.

I should make it clear that while this story is about the development of Alaska tourism, it was not "tours" that kept us in business during those early years. Arctic Alaska Travel was to become a highly successful and profitable retail travel agency. Our bread-and-butter customers were Fairbanks residents who traveled "Outside" on business and vacations. It was the retail travel agency branch of the business that supported me and my family and provided a financial base for the Alaska tour operation —

which grew steadily but was not self-sustaining until 1951 when we opened a Seattle office.

One day during that first summer, two lady school teachers from the South 48 showed up at the office on First Avenue. They wanted to go sight seeing. Could I recommend someone? I asked what they wanted to see. "Whatever is of interest," they responded. "We want to see the Fairbanks sights." At the time, my personal car was a 1936 Plymouth sedan in reasonable condition. Not wanting to turn down an opportunity to make a dollar, I agreed to take the two ladies on a tour.

I found a lot to show them. Fairbanks is another of many Alaskan communities that started with a gold rush. In 1902 an Italian prospector named Felix Pedro discovered gold on what is now called Pedro Creek, twelve miles north of the present-day city center. Gold rush stampedes in 1903 and 1904 brought in thousands of miners and assorted adventurers. Within a few years the gold rush town became the trading and communications center of northern Alaska. Today, Fairbanks, with a population of about 40,000, is the second largest city in Alaska — tourism is a major industry. Modern, wide-window, tinted glass, 47-passenger motorcoaches take hundreds of sightseers on tours daily.

But on a June day in 1947, that 47-passenger motorcoach was a 1936 Plymouth, and the total number of sightseers touring Fairbanks was two. We saw the University and the University Museum, toured the Farmers' Loop, and went to the municipal gardens. We inspected log-built St. Matthews Episcopal Church, which burned down later that same year but has since been restored. I told the ladies about the land, the climate and life in the Arctic. I enjoyed the role of guide and raconteur. We saw the confluence of the Chena and Tanana rivers and dwellings of local residents, including log cabins built during gold rush days. Many of those early structures are still seen today in "Alaskaland," a commemorative park established in 1967 for the Alaska Centennial. We also found, picked, and ate some wild blueberries, and went to a small farm where we pulled Alaska radishes from the ground, and washed and ate them — large, firm and juicy. Besides looking at Alaska, we tasted and smelled it.

The ladies had a grand time. So did I — even though the Plymouth had a flat tire and we were all three nearly eaten alive by mosquitoes. Back at their hotel, they asked what they owed me.

I didn't know. "This is the first time I ever did anything like this," I explained. "What do you think it's worth?"

They suggested $10 from each of them.

"Sounds fine to me," I agreed.

They handed me a $20 bill and my lightning-quick calculator mind went to work: two people in a car, $20; five people in a car, $50. I hustled back to the office to explain a new plan to the staff.

"We're going into the sightseeing business," I enthused. "We'll charge ten dollars a person and try to get at least three or four signed up before we take the tour — extra income, more people walking through the door."

We lettered a butcher paper sign for the office window: "SIGHTSEEING $10."

And it took about three days before an outraged local taxicab operator, Joe Coble of Yellow Cab, showed up to inform me — belligerently — that I couldn't do that.

My belligerence matched his: "Why can't I?"

His answer was a snarl: "You don't have a license. You've got to have a "For Hire" license and a taxi license, too. We're handling the sightseeing in this town. We have an exclusive charter for it."

I wanted to know who conducted his tours. He told me his drivers did. That wasn't my day for euphemism: "They're a bunch of drunks, drifters, and no goods. They shouldn't be representing Alaska."

I offered Coble a proposition: If he would train drivers to operate sightseeing tours properly, I would represent him. His answer was, "Get out of the business; we're handling it." The fight was on, albeit a short one. I went to the Fairbanks City Council and asked what I had to do to get a "For Hire" license. "Buy one," they told me, and they explained that if I didn't want to be classified as a taxi service and be on call 24 hours a day, I could operate with a simple "For Hire" license. As easy as that, I went into the sightseeing business legally and immediately.

Then, once again, The Prince of Serendip was at my side. Walking down a Fairbanks street that day, I spotted — parked in front of Lavery's Market — a brand new DeSoto Suburban, a big eight-passenger car, upholstered in white vinyl, elegantly finished in gold and brown, and topped off with chrome luggage racks. I took one look and no ten-year-old kid ever wanted a fire engine more than I wanted that DeSoto. A man sat at the wheel (waiting for his wife in the market). I expressed my admiration for his car and inquired if he would consider selling it. He would! He was an automobile dealer; selling cars was his business. An omen. He wanted $4,500, a lot of money in 1947, more than I wanted to spend, perhaps more than I *should* have spent. But I *had* to have the DeSoto; I was sure it would be the making of our new sightseeing business.

The auto dealer agreed to take my 1936 Plymouth in trade ("If it's stout enough to pull a trailer"). He wanted $3,500 to boot. My bank arranged a loan to be paid in one year. I asked the dealer to throw in a gray tweed suit I had seen hanging in the back of the car. He was about my size and I needed a new suit. He laughed, threw up his hands — and threw in the suit. (When a dealer meets a dealer one of them must give way.)

The car ran fine, it was Marguerite who blew a gasket. At some length she reminded me — when I proudly drove the DeSoto home — of the uncertainties of our circumstances and of my family responsibilities: "I know you love cars, but this time you've gone too far." But as soon as I explained the new sightseeing idea, she recognized its value. And as it turned out, the idea was valid. We bought the DeSoto in 1947. Next year we added a new Chrysler limousine to accommodate our growing sightseeing business, and in 1949 two more.

Meanwhile, I was becoming aware that my miserable First Avenue office wouldn't do. No longer was I selling tickets on the non-sched airlines. That idea had brought in dollars during a critical period — but high class promotion it wasn't.

Our office location became an issue when I went to Pan American and proposed that I be appointed a Pan Am agent. As an exclusive Northwest Airlines agent, I had been a Pan American competitor. When I told the Pan American people that I could bring them business, they assured me they didn't need an agent; they already had their own office in Fairbanks.

"You *do* need me," I insisted. "I know the people around here better than your sales representatives can ever hope to know them."

That's when the office location came up — in their words, ". . . your, uh, 'office' . . . it isn't really what one might consider being even close to adequate."

For the time being, my proposal to represent Pan American would have to wait.

People used to say: "It isn't *what* you know, it's *who* you know." In today's jargon that's called "networking" — people talking to people, sharing knowledge, information, resources. Whatever you call it, it was a tool I had learned to use with facility. I had ideas, knew people, and enjoyed a happy gift for eliciting their help and cooperation.

Into my office one day walked an acquaintance — Captain Austin E. Lathrop, former steamboat captain and a well-known Fairbanks entrepreneur who had made a fortune in building, banking and coal. Lathrop owned many of the principal buildings in Fairbanks: Empress Theater, Lacey Theater Building, Bank of Fairbanks, Lathrop Building. He also owned the radio station (KFAR) which broadcast my weekly aviation show.

Standing in the doorway the captain surveyed my graceless First Avenue quarters. Obviously, he had something on his mind. He asked what my ambitions were for my business. I told him I wanted to build a tour company and expand from Arctic excursions to tours throughout Alaska, and to extend my sightseeing operation to include other Alaskan cities.

To the good Captain a spade was a spade, and a crummy office was a crummy office: "You're not going to make it down here," he growled.

"You've got to have a better location. How would you like to be up on Second Avenue."

I told him I would like it just fine, but I didn't know of any place on Second Avenue I could afford: "I don't want to get overextended and see the whole operation go bust."

Lathrop suggested that I let *him* worry about that. Come and see me next week," he counseled. "We may have something to talk about."

The captain's Empress Theater Building was one of the choice properties in downtown Fairbanks. On the street side of the building, a prime office space had been leased to Skinner & Eddy, owners of Alaska Steamship Company. The Captain — after explaining to Alaska Steam that I was in the travel business but not a competitor — arranged for me to have a desk in their office with one girl to provide office help. I made the move quickly that August.

Within three years *I* had the office, and Alaska Steam was doing business from the single desk.

Cap Lathrop never realized a dime's profit from Arctic Alaska Travel Service. He was a money maker but he didn't find it necessary to profit directly from every business contact he made. He helped me because he liked me and because he had a generous spirit. He also gave me some sage advice: "Chuck, you'll be successful in business if you always take care to surround yourself with people of equal or better ability than your own. You're bringing a new industry to Alaska and with your ideas and energy you should do very well. But you must have the right people, the very best that you can find."

Connections By Sea

A great mountain chain fringes the Alaskan coastline from the tip of the Southeast panhandle to Western Alaska, a distance of more than 1,200 miles. Without going there to see it, one cannot comprehend the impenetrability of this mountain barrier: its jagged peaks, glaciers, roaring rivers, muskeg swamps and winter cold.

Only the irresistible lure of gold could breach that wilderness rampart. Along the entire 1,200 miles there are still today only four surface routes leading from the coast across the mountains to the interior. Three of these started as gold rush trails. The fourth is the Alaska Railroad, completed in 1920 and paralleled today by the George Parks Highway.

Although the gold rushers were not the first to reach the interior, they were the first to cross the mountains in any numbers. Those who preceded them had followed the Yukon River from its headwaters in western Canada or its outlet at St. Michael on the Bering Sea. As early as 1847 Hudson's Bay Company had established a fur trading outpost at Fort Yukon where the river intersects the Arctic Circle. In 1869, a small American riverboat, the *Youkon*, steamed inland from St. Michael, carrying fur traders who established trading posts along the river. By the early 1880s prospectors had explored large parts of Alaska, many of them finding gold — although in small quantities compared to the great gold strikes that came later in the Klondike and at Fairbanks, Nome, and other points.

In 1883, fifteen years before the Klondike stampede, U.S. Army officer Frederick Schwatka made his way across Chilkoot Pass from Dyea near Skagway and surveyed the Yukon by floating down river on a raft. This was the route followed by many thousands of stampeders in the gold rush of 1897-98. A few miles to the west, thousands more — also Klondike bound — trudged the Dalton Trail over Chilkat Pass.

At the same time, still farther west, at Valdez on an arm of Prince William Sound, some three thousand more stampeders endured terrible hardships trying to discover an "all American" route across Valdez Glacier and through the Chugach Mountain Range to the gold fields. Few made it. Many perished. But a safe passage from Valdez was discovered in 1899 by Captain W. R. Abercrombie of the U.S. Army. His route became known as the Abercrombie Trail and was used to construct a telegraph line to Eagle, another gold rush community far to the north on the Yukon River.

Later, in 1905, after the Fairbanks gold rush, a second trail was explored, connecting with Abercrombie's trail at Gakona, 130 miles inland from Valdez. This second trail crossed the Alaska Range to Fairbanks. Gradually, the two trails evolved into a wagon road, then into a stage coach route, and by the 1920s into an automobile road — the Richardson Highway.

Perhaps the most famous of the historic routes to the interior was the narrow-gauge White Pass & Yukon Route railroad completed in 1900 from Skagway to Whitehorse where it connected with Yukon riverboats to the Klondike.

By 1947, when I was just beginning to ferret out the components of an Alaska tour industry, the mountain barrier that had inflicted terrible hardships a half century earlier was potentially Alaska's greatest tourist attraction. Each of the old gold rush trails was to become an important tourist route between the coast and the interior.

Before the war Alaska Steamship Company had offered tours by rail and motorcoach from the coast across the mountains to Fairbanks. These tours connected with ships from Seattle which called at Valdez and also at Seward on Kenai Peninsula south of Anchorage. Ship passengers who disembarked at Seward rode the Alaska Railroad north to Fairbanks and returned via the Richardson Highway to Valdez where they reboarded a ship for the southbound voyage back to Seattle. The "horseshoe" routing crossed the Alaska Range twice and followed the Abercrombie Trail through the Chugach Range. The map facing the *CONTENTS* page gives a clearer picture of this overland tour and how it connected with ship routes.

I envisioned reestablishing this rail-highway-ship connection and talked to D. E. Skinner of Skinner & Eddy Company, which in 1944 had assumed control of Alaska Steam from Kennecott Copper. Skinner suggested that I see Alaska Steam's general traffic manager, a man named Peterson. When I met Peterson he wanted reassurance that passengers would not be stuck in Anchorage or Fairbanks without suitable accommodations. I told him I would take responsibility — make up the beds myself, if necessary.

I must have been convincing because Peterson bought the idea, and in July of 1947 I introduced post-war "Golden Belt Line" tours. The horseshoe route could be traveled in either direction: from Seward to Valdez via Fairbanks or from Valdez to Seward via Fairbanks. The Seward-Fairbanks leg was by rail with overnight stops at Anchorage, Curry, and Mt. McKinley National Park. The Valdez-Fairbanks leg was by bus on the Richardson Highway with overnights at Copper Center and other roadhouses along the way. The entire tour took seven days and meshed with the sailings of Alaska Steam, which at that time operated four passenger vessels between Seattle and Seward — *Baranof, Aleutian, Alaska* and *Denali.*

Today, similar packages that combine sea voyages with land tours of the interior account for the overwhelming majority of Alaska tour routings. Neither land tours alone nor cruises alone can convey the monumental scope of Alaska's mountains, rivers, islands, tidewater glaciers, tundra meadows, forests and wildlife.

From Seward our Golden Belt Line rail route was to Anchorage where the train circles Knik Arm, a long tidal inlet, before crossing the Matanuska Valley, Alaska's agricultural center. After leaving the coastal region the train follows the Susitna River into the Alaska Range, with frequent views (weather permitting) of Mt. McKinley. After skirting Mt. McKinley National Park (renamed Denali National Park and Preserve in 1981) the train winds down the northern flank of the Alaska Range to Fairbanks.

The Richardson Highway, which crosses both the Alaska Range and the Chugach Range between Valdez and Fairbanks, is considered by many Alaskans to be the most beautiful motor route in the North. During the gold rush era roadhouses sprang up a day's wagon journey apart along the old trail. Several of these picturesque, log-built waystops are still in use, providing coffee and luncheon breaks for the big, tinted-window motor-coaches that nowadays carry travelers from Valdez to Fairbanks in a single day (363 miles). In 1947 that drive took two days. The old-time roadhouses provided overnight accommodations as well as coffee and meals. One of our overnights was at Copper Center, a historic hotel built as a trading post in 1896, predating the gold rush — and in continuous operation ever since. Others were located at Gulkana and Tonsina. Though rustic they were warm and comfortable. Originally, these lodges were for travelers who went by horse-drawn wagons in summer and by sleighs and sledges in winter. some had individual bedrooms, some offered only separate dormitories for men and women. Copper Center Lodge, operated by pioneer Alaskans George and Kathy Ashby, was the best of the lot with the most modern facilities. George passed away several years ago; Kathy remains at Copper Center, taking care of the lodge as in the past.

By modern standards, travel on Alaskan roads in 1947 was still primitive. To carry my passengers between Fairbanks and Valdez, I first used scheduled bus service by O'Hara Bus Lines, centered in Gulkana on the Richardson Highway. But the bus company soon went out of business and I began to charter 33-passenger Beck buses from a Fairbanks businessman, Paul Greimann, a Chrysler-Plymouth dealer who also owned University

Bus Lines. On dirt and gravel roads — there was no paving of any kind — trips were slow and uncomfortable. Parts of the trip were downright hazardous. At one sharp curve in a mountain pass, drivers had to back and fill two or three times to negotiate a twist in the road. On one side was a solid granite wall, on the other a sheer dropoff, where a miscue could have sent the bus plummeting hundreds of feet into a gorge.

Buses were not equipped with restrooms, and roadside facilities were primitive — most highway rest stops had outdoor privies. One of these was called Tiekel and the driver always got a laugh when he announced to his passengers, "We're going to tinkle at Tiekel!" The Tiekel stop was unusual in that the privies were built out over the rushing waters of a wilderness stream. Environmental and pollution controls were nonexistent in those days. The women's privy was some distance upstream from the men's, but the shrieks and giggles of the "girls" were clearly heard when their nether regions were baptized by icy spray thrown up from the rushing wilderness stream striking the rocks below.

Not only were roadside facilities primitive, they were also widely spaced through the Alaskan wilderness. When passengers became uncomfortable someone was sure to shout, "Hey! It's time for a rest stop!" The accommodating driver would find a stretch of road where trees and brush grew high on either side and announce: "Men to the left, women to the right." Passengers would pour off the bus and the driver would wait for about ten minutes until they came straggling back out of the trees, beating off mosquitoes. I believe that no one can fully appreciate the mosquito unless one has made a roadside "rest stop" in the Alaskan bush!

But even though accommodations and roads were primitive, customers seldom complained. They accepted frontier conditions — the dust, mosquitoes, and brambles. They came to Alaska expecting to rough it, and they weren't disappointed when they encountered what they had expected.

That first year, we sold 127 of those "Golden Belt Line" tours, primarily through travel agents in West Coast cities.

Looking back, I find it interesting to observe how many of the elements of modern-day Alaska tourism were "in place" by the end of our first season (1947), less than a year after my separation from Wien. True — those elements were rudimentary, but the skeleton was there, waiting to be filled out: we were taking air tours to the Arctic; we had started city sightseeing; we were operating highway tours between major cities; we had tested the beginnings of the "cruise tour" concept — packaging tours that connected with passenger ships at Seward and Valdez. We had even begun to package the rail-motorcoach trip from Skagway — northern port of the Inside Passage

— to Whitehorse, Fairbanks, McKinley Park and Anchorage. This latter tour is still today the bread and butter of the entire Alaska tour industry. All this happened in one short season. And it was a profitable season to boot, a matter of considerable satisfaction to myself, to Marguerite, and to our respective families.

Days went by in a blur of activity. Almost everything we did was new and untested. We were inventing, operating, experimenting, changing — all at the same time. And for the most part, we had the satisfaction of seeing our ideas and systems work. Most of our customers — in fact, almost all of our customers — went home happy. We had delivered what we had promised to deliver, and the magnificence of Alaska took care of the rest.

Although tourists knew that Alaska lacked the amenities, we did have a few customers who complained — and of course we remember the few complainers more than the many friendly people who came to see a new part of the world, quietly enjoyed it, and went home happy. I recall the man who showed up one day in my office, a picture of sartorial elegance — brushed gray derby hat, dark suit, and a noticeable layer of dust smudging the gleam of his polished shoes.

"Mr. West," he began, "I want you to know that I'm not happy." When I inquired why, he explained that no matter how hard he tried, he could not keep his shoes clean. I wasn't sure what he wanted me to do about that. Fairbanks had only one paved street, and that lonely piece of contrete — the only pavement north of Anchorage — was just one block long. Everything else was dirt and gravel. I tried to explain that Alaska, even Fairbanks, was still frontier. My explanation was inadequate. He went away not much happier than when he had come in — but he went away.

And once a lady traveler arrived who wanted all kinds of extra attention right from the start. Heavily made up, she wore high heels, an expensive fur coat, a sexy dress — and she cuddled in her hand one of those tiny Mexican Chihuahua dogs, duded up in a fancy little collar. She had arrived in late October after the first snow had fallen.

When we stopped at the woman's hotel, she put her wee dog down on the sidewalk while she dug for something in her purse. Just then a dog team — Huskies, Malemutes and mixed breeds — came running full tilt down the street pulling a sled. In those days dog teams were a common sight in Fairbanks, but that Chihuahua had never seen anything like it before and when the sled team rounded the corner into sight the little mutt made a serious error in judgment. He bounced stiff legged out into the street and began snarling and yipping. The team's lead dog, an Alaskan Malemute that weighed at least ninety pounds, decided snack time had arrived early that day. Without even breaking stride, he scooped up the little Chihuahua and with one mighty crunch bit the pooch in two. The third dog back grabbed a tidbit from mid-air, and by the time the team had passed (fortunately, it all happened quickly), the lady's Chihuahua was but a memory. She stood on the curb, petrified by the macabre sight she had just witnessed. Then she began to shriek, "Fifi! My Fifi!"

It was one of those times when one hardly knows what to say.

And once, a Fairbanks woman, a local resident, booked transportation to the Midwest to attend a funeral. During her trip she missed a travel connection and the funeral as well. She blamed Arctic Alaska Travel and she phoned her husband, a local Fairbanks attorney, who in turn phoned me. There was no doubt in my mind that the lawyer was drunk when he made the call. His telephone conversation deteriorated rapidly into earthy name calling — which distressed me sorely. I reciprocated and accused him of being a coward for hiding his abuse at the end of a telephone.

A few minutes later the man showed up in our office, this time punctuating his invective by stabbing the air with a pistol. Trying not to reveal my consternation, I said, "First you hide behind a telephone and now you hide behind a gun." I turned to one of the frightened girls in the office, Harriett Forbes, and told her to call the police. Then I told the attorney what I was going to do with that pistol if he didn't put it away. Fortunately, he was bluffable. He hesitated and then stalked out of the office. We reported the incident to the police and preferred charges against the man for assault with a deadly weapon. Following a hearing, the offender spent three days in jail. The police suggested to me that perhaps I hadn't shown good judgment in trying to face down an armed man who might have been deranged enough to pull the trigger. I didn't mention to them that keeping my temper under control has never been one of my strong points. Under the circumstances I didn't know what else I could have done. Harriett Forbes later became a travel agent in Aberdeen, Washington. She recalls the incident whenever we meet.

Another less than cordial scene occurred one night in the Cottage Bar over a nearby stationery store. A Seattle-based firm had opened a Fairbanks office during the period when travel to Seattle via the non-scheduled airlines was at its peak. The firm's chief representative let it be known that he wasn't about to give an upstart such as Arctic Alaska Travel so much as breathing room. That night in the Cottage Bar he became more boastful and abusive — of me — with every drink. The gist of his commentary was that he and his company were going to "run that son-of-a-bitch Chuck West right out of town."

As it happened, a friend of mine who was seated in the next booth hustled over to my office (night work was the rule in those busy times) and related to me the tenor of my new competitor's remarks. Not being one to take a circuitous or indirect route when a face down would serve at least as well, I locked up shop and hiked over to the Cottage Bar. My frame of mind was such that the man's six-inch height advantage, with weight to match, made little difference to me. After introductory remarks, I told him I could take him physically, mentally, financially, or any other way he might suggest. The irony of the situation warmed my ire: while I was working late in the office building my business, he was drinking and bragging in a bar about building his. I suggested that if he was sincere about running me out of town, he could start right now by stepping outside. The man didn't even get out of his seat. He later went to jail for embezzlement, and his company went out of business the following year.

Tent City — Trying to Find Hotels

During the winter of 1947-48 a newspaperman, Paul Solka, with the Fairbanks *News-Miner*, helped me write, lay out, and print a folder describing our Arctic tours. This was mailed to West Coast travel agents. That same winter I made a sales trip down the West Coast to call on agents and tell them about what was happening in Alaska. The preceding year had seen the Arctic Coast tours to Nome and Kotzebue work out as I had hoped. It also saw the beginning of a city sightseeing operation in Fairbanks and the start of highway tours through the Alaska interior. All of these ventures showed promise. I looked forward with optimism to the 1948 season.

The structure of Arctic Alaska Tours evolved gradually. The company was well conceived and would endure — but the growing wasn't easy. The years 1947 through 1954 were a madcap logistical scramble to arrange transportation on anything that moved and to secure lodging and provide food service for incoming visitors — all the while coping with the whims of weather, maritime unions, crowded facilities, inadequate roadways, and frontier accommodations. Life was a difficult, wonderful, never-to-be-forgotten three-ring circus. We managed to keep most of our customers happy most of the time, though, as we shall see, not all of them were happy all of the time . . .

In 1948 Alaska boomed with new construction — Ladd Air Force Base, Eielson Air Force Base, also oil exploration on the North Slope. Hotels and boarding houses bulged with cat skinners, welders, carpenters, crane operators, mechanics. Fairbanks had run out of rooms, and with a busy tourist season approaching, I anticipated problems finding space for tourist travelers. After casting about for answers — any answer — to this dilemma, I settled on what I thought was a solution. I would build a "Tent City!"

In a new subdivision south of town, at Sixteenth and Cushman, was a piece of land 180 feet deep that boasted 200 feet of highway frontage. I negotiated a loan and also a partnership with a local banker, Phil Johnson, to finance purchase of this strip. (Only in Alaska would a banker become partner with a bank customer. In the South 48 this would have been a questionable business practice.)

We graded the land and set about buying war-surplus squad tents, stoves, beds, mattresses. The truth is that I didn't know what I was doing in this venture, but paying passengers woud soon arrive and I had to put them *somewhere*. We drilled a well and hired a construction foreman to supervise building of boardwalks, tent frames, and a utility building with showers, toilets and wash basins. Then we hired a resident manager and his wife, Bill and Sue Merritt, to help look after the tourists. By early July when the tourist season peaked and we were frantic for rooms, we thought we had anticipated everything our customers would need. Tent City opened for business.

The first tourists *and a hard summer rain* arrived on the same day, closely followed by more grief than Arctic Alaska Tours could ever have foreseen. We had erected ten tents that were intended to sleep four people each. (I had the mistaken notion that strangers wouldn't mind sharing a tent — scratch another idea that wouldn't work.)

And the squabble over sharing tents was a mere nothing compared to what followed. My 180x200-foot property metamorphosed into a 180x200-foot mudhole. Alaska is known for its muskeg swamps. But in July of 1948 the largest and deepest swamp in the Territory was located at Sixteenth and Cushman, Fairbanks. I swear.

Tents leaked. Firewood smoked or refused to burn at all. Bumpy mattresses smelled of mildew. Restaurants were far away. For the solace of a mere hot cup of coffee, my good customers braved wind, rain and mud, making their way into town by whatever conveyance they could find.

And then there were the mosquitoes.

Although my previous customers had been tolerant of frontier conditions, this was asking too much. My Tent City established an all-time record for discontent. With my high hopes for a profitable season sinking into a 180x200-foot quagmire, I became known around town as the "Tenthouse King." Oldtimers still remember.

I had to do something, *anything* and went into town where I bared my soul to Grace Hagberg, owner of the Fairbanks Hotel, a three-story walk-up accommodation:

"Mrs. Hagberg," I implored, "I'm desperate. I have some half-drowned cheechakos in tents at Sixteenth and Cushman, and they're ready to riot if I don't do something for them." I asked her if she would rent me all the rooms on the top floor of her hotel for the rest of the summer. I told her I would pay for the rooms in advance.

The lady liberated the cheechakos from the swamp and extracted a budding young entrepreneur from serious trouble. Although the Fairbanks Hotel wasn't the swankiest in town, my tourists — after staying at Tent City — thought they had gone to heaven. For the first time in days I breathed easy.

There was another Fairbanks lady who provided an invaluable service during those early years. Mrs. Eva McGowan — Irish, cheerful, gregarious — managed the Fairbanks Chamber of Commerce housing bureau that had been established during war years to alleviate an acute room shortage. Mrs. McGown operated from a desk in the lobby of the Nordale Hotel. If rooms weren't available at any of the hotels she almost always could place travelers in one or another of the private homes with rooms to let. She waited at her desk until the last night train, sometimes into the small hours of the morning, to help stranded passengers find accommodations.

She was a wonder. Many times she helped my people find a place to stay when I was sure every bed in town was full — the hotel situation was impossible. Often, to help Mrs. McGowan, I provided ground transporation, delivering travelers to their accommodations in the DeSoto or the Chrysler limousines that came after them, or on occasion in my own car. The prime directive was to get the weary, sometimes ill-tempered travelers bedded down for the night. Almost always, we succeeded.

A sad footnote to Eva McGowan's story was written when the Nordale Hotel burned in the late sixties. The irrepressible lady perished in that fire.

If it is true, as they say, that we learn from our mistakes, the Tent City fiasco made me Solomon. We were better prepared for 1949. Wooden barracks on a former government housing site across the Chena River had been declared surplus; and Arctic Alaska Tours, in partnership with banker Phil Johnson, bought them. We sliced the buildings into manageable sections and when the river froze that winter dragged them across the ice to be reassembled at Sixteenth and Cushman.

Gutting the wartime housing modules, we rebuilt the interiors and reassembled the sections in the form of an "H," reserving the center section for a manager's apartment and guests' showers, toilets and utility rooms. The single-story wooden building became the first tourist hotel in Alaska — the first hotel built solely to accommodate vacationing travelers and sightseers. We named it the Tanana Court and opened in spring 1949.

Recalling our disaster one year earlier, we arranged to serve continental breakfasts in the lobby — coffee, juice, doughnuts, and fresh cinnamon rolls. The hotel also provided transportation into town so that our guests might choose among local restaurants for noon and evening meals.

In years to come Mr. and Mrs. Kenneth Friske became partners in this operation, serving as resident managers of the small, clean hotel. Eventually, I bought out my partners and as Fairbanks grew the Tanana Court grew with the community to become the Fairbanks Inn — a modern facility completely surrounded by the city.

Having our own small hotel was only a partial answer to the Fairbanks bed shortage; the scramble to find space at other accommodations continued. I was in good physical condition in those days. Many of my little lady travelers couldn't manage their own luggage and few hotels sported bellmen. Carrying luggage up several flights of stairs day after day and night after night built my stamina. Besides acting as entrepreneur and agency manager, and filling in as tour guide and driver — I was also a porter. Eventually, it all got to be too much for me and I hired a young college student, Brad Phillips, to help.

Today, hotels in major Alaska cities are as modern and comfortable as fine hotels anywhere, but during the late '40s and into the '50s, Alaska hotels, even the best of them, were "pre-war frontier." Inevitably, a few of our customers could not understand this and were hard to please.

There's an interesting chemistry that can take place within a group of travelers who share the same hotel, bus, or sightseeing trip. On occasion, just one person or more often a couple can "poison" an entire group, infecting everyone else in the group with their sourpuss outlook. Some people go through life that way.

Another kind of traveler is the person, or couple, that is perfectly content with an accommodation until they learn that someone else in the group has what they feel is better, not unlike the small child who is happy with a medium-sided piece of cake until another child across the table receives a slightly larger piece. And while these annoying travelers plague the tour industry all around the world, they were at times especially difficult in early-day Alaska. Experience taught me that the only answer for these peole was simply to face them straightforwardly and tell them: "This is the way it is."

One morning (the year was 1950) at about 3:00 a.m., Brad Phillips called me at home. One of the buses had suffered a mishap on the highway and was delayed, arriving in Fairbanks well after midnight. A small party of women passengers was complaining to Brad about the rooms reserved for them. He had been up since 6:00 a.m. and was at his wits' end when he telephoned. Would I please come down to the hotel and fix things? Yes, I would.

I climbed into my clothes and drove to the hotel where I found a harried Brad Phillips and, as reported, the disgruntled women fuming and sitting on their suitcases. They refused to budge. I said to Brad, "You go home. You've been up long enough." Then I turned to the ladies and told them how things were. I said, "I'm the boss and I want you to know that you have two choices. You can let me take your bags up to your rooms and you can go to bed and get some rest. Or you can sit here on your bags for the rest of the night. There are simply no more rooms in this town. I'm going to wait three minutes for you to make up your minds, then I'm leaving. What do you want to do?''

Well, it didn't take three minutes. I lugged their bags up the stairs and got them tucked in. Then I went home. The next morning they came into the office to apologize for causing all that trouble. They had been tired and out-of-sorts and had not been able to make the best of a less-than-ideal situation. It worked out fine in the end.

There was another time when push-came-to-shove, and I shoved. I had gone to the railroad station to pick up a family — a man, his wife, and two grown children. The man demanded to know where their hotel reservations were. He wanted their luggage left at the station until he learned where they would stay the night. He — ''certainly didn't want to stay at the Nordale Hotel.'' I informed him that his reservations were at the Nordale. He told me not to move the bags: ''I'm not going to permit my family to put up at the likes of the Nordale.'' I told him the reservations had been held in his name for a long time and that at 9:30 at night there was no way they could be changed. He demanded a complete refund on *all* his arrangements made by Arctic Alaska Tours. I told him to see me in my office the next morning and that I would refund — ''every dime you've paid me. But as of this moment, as I understand it, you're canceling your tour?'' He barked confirmation, That was all I needed to hear. I reached down, pulled the Arctic Alaska Tours baggage tags from their luggage, got in the limousine, drove to the Nordale, canceled their reservations, told the desk clerk to sell their space to someone else, and then called Pan American and canceled their reservation on their flight to Seattle the next day.

We learned later that with the help of Mrs. McGowan the man finally found lodging about midnight in a rooming house. When he went to Pan Am the following day and learned that his reservations had been canceled, he protested that *he* had not canceled them. The airline reservations clerk replied, ''Yes, but Chuck West did.''

We tried our best to be courteous, friendly, and accommodating — but sometimes, with some people . . . well . . .

And Fairbanks wasn't the only city in Alaska with a room shortage. Because more and more visitors were taking our Arctic Coast excursions, we were outgrowing available beds in Kotzebue. These tours had triggered our entire enterprise and were still an important component in the package of services that we offered our customers.

In 1949 Wien Air got the first of several DC-3s. Equipped with regular passenger seats instead of the fold-down metal bucket seats our Arctic passengers had been using, the new aircraft were ideally suited for our Arctic Coast excursions, a great improvement over the non-sched charters. Wien had also obtained a new FAA-certificated route from Fairbanks to Kotzebue.

I had learned by now that chartering non-sched aircraft could be an uncertain business; certificated operators were more dependable. I went to Wien with the suggestion that Arctic Alaska Tours abandon the charters and use his DC-3s instead. We would sell the tours; he would operate the aircraft.

Wien bought the idea and, beginning that season, flights that were sold through Arctic Alaska Tours departed Fairbanks every day of the week on Wien's airplanes. I was vindicated in my earlier boasts that I would make more money for Wien Airlines with my own tour business than by working for him directly and flying his airplanes.

For Arctic Alaska, Kotzebue was a good-sized community, numbering some 800 people. We had used rooms in Archie Ferguson's store-restaurant-roadhouse. And though his place was clean, warm, pleasant, and well run, we were about to outgrow it, along with another store-hotel in town — Louie Rotman's. What to do?

In 1950 a dormitory building that had been used to house workmen who built Kotzebue Airport came up for sale. I felt it could be converted into an acceptable hotel and suggested to the Wiens that they buy the building — they would need hotel space to support their certificated route into Kotzebue. They agreed, providing I would help them finance it.

I also suggested that Wien take over Kotzebue ground services — transfers, sightseeing — from Arctic Alaska Tours. Again, they agreed and brought in Frank Whaley to manage this for them. Whaley had been Wien's most celebrated bush pilot, awarded the United States Air Force "Air Medal" for rescuing the crew of a downed B-29 in an Arctic snowstorm. In Kotzebue he developed and expanded tourist facilities and services, bringing in needed buses and automobiles, and keeping a close watch over visitors' needs during their stay.

In most parts of the world the tour operator is concerned almost exclusively with the packaging, sale and booking of tours. The separate components that make up the tours — lodging, sightseeing, transportation — are already in place, available for "assembly" by the tour operator as needed. In busy post-war Alaska the tour "components" weren't there. With every new city that we added to our tour itineraries, I had to scramble to find hotel space. Fairbanks and Kotzebue were examples.

And hotels were only a piece of the total picture. Motorcoach transportation is a separate chapter. . . .

Motorcoaches And Riverboats

In many parts of the world the traveler's interest focuses on major cities. London, Paris and Rome are more important than the spaces between. In Alaska the reverse is true. Glaciers, mountains, a moose swimming a river, an eagle soaring over a salmon stream — these are what the traveler comes to see. And while it is true that a colorful history and frontier spirit flavor Alaska's cities and towns, it is the great wilderness between that draws modern-day explorers to the North Country.

Logistically speaking, this translates into a need for highway transportation — buses. I first needed buses when we introduced post-war "Golden Belt Line" tours on the Richardson Highway betwen Fairbanks and Valdez. In those days ground transportation was primitive by South 48 standards. We made do with what we could improvise in a catch-as-catch-can world.

For our service on the Richardson Highway, we were chartering buses from University Bus Lines, an urban transit service in Fairbanks owned by Paul Greimann. I knew Greimann to be an experienced, successful operator. Besides his bus business, he owned a Chrysler-Plymouth dealership and a garage with a crew of mechanics. Confident that his company would mesh well with Arctic Alaska Tours, I asked him how he felt about expanding the bus charter operation on the Richardson Highway.

Greimann liked the idea and bought additional units of a newer model Beck. He also agreed to change the name of his company from "University Bus Lines" to "Alaska Coachways" — and to paint the buses with the State of Alaska colors, blue and gold. We formed a cooperative enterprise that endured several years.

Arctic Alaska Tours arranged all bookings on Greimann's highway buses, scheduling runs so that the same bus that delivered embarking Alaska Steam passengers at Valdez also picked up incoming passengers bound for Fairbanks. Sometimes, buses had to "deadhead" (run empty) to Valdez to meet arriving passengers, but usually they were full both ways.

At the time I was flying a Super Cub. When ships docked at Valdez, I flew down from Fairbanks, met with the purser, assigned passengers to their buses, and phoned ahead to tell roadhouse managers how many people to expect. Then I dispatched the bus drivers, scooted out to my airplane and, while my travelers marvelled at Keystone Canyon and Horsetail Falls, flew ahead to the roadhouse airstrip and was there to meet the same people I had dispatched earlier from Valdez.

One night I stayed at Copper Center Lodge, parking the Super Cub on the grass field. Next morning I took off for Fairbanks to be there when travelers arrived. I ran into "weather" at Summit Lake near Isabel Pass and couldn't get through the mountains. Turning back, I landed on the road, parked the plane at a gravel pit turnout, and hitched a ride on a passing tanker truck. In spite of the delay I still got to Fairbanks in time to go home and change my clothes before going downtown to meet the buses. That night we ran out of beds. I managed to find accommodations for the last couple in a private home and personally drove them there in my car. Discovering that the landlady wasn't quite ready for us, I helped her make the bed.

My tourist couple couldn't get over it. The man said, "Young fellow, I don't know how you do it. I've seen you everywhere along the route. I saw you on the dock at Valdez, at the lodge in Copper Center, you met us in Fairbanks, and now you're making our bed." When he wanted to tip me I explained that accepting tips was not company policy and that we wanted to do everything possible to make their stay comfortable.

Next morning the same man walked into our office while I was waiting on customers. "So you run the office, as well," he said.

"Yes, and I sweep out at night, too."

"You're the boss, right?"

"Right."

The rear-engined Beck buses were usually dependable but like all mechanical equipment occasionally demanded extra care. On one trip the carburetor came loose from the intake manifold. We were carrying a group of travelers sent by a South 48 company, Scenery Unlimited Tours, and escorted by a man named Howard Hansen. The driver prevailed on him to help out in the emergency. By sitting on the rear seat of the bus, he could just manage to reach over into the engine compartment and hold the carburetor secure on top of the intake manifold. Years later, Hansen was to join Arctic Alaska Tours' successor — Westours — and eventually he became vice president of sales for that company.

All buses carried first-aid equipment. If this proved inadequate for an emergency, ill or injured passengers were taken to the nearest home, way station or highway facility that had an airstrip, and then flown by bush plane to more sophisticated medical facilities.

Once, all these contingency measures were no help. In the middle of nowhere, a man died suddenly of a heart attack or stroke. Our only option was to continue on — carrying the deceased, a coat over his head, to the next destination.

My association with Paul Greimann proved invaluable: he knew the bus business — and was also a resourceful man in an emergency, as I was to learn one night during the winter of 1948-49 when he and I were driving from Fairbanks to Anchorage in my DeSoto. We were going to Anchorage to explore the possibility of establishing a joint office there.

On a bright moonlight night with the temperature 65 degrees below zero — cold enough to make rubber brittle — a tire went flat on the Glenn Highway southwest of Tok. I had a spare. We changed the tire. My God, but 65 below is cold! As we got back into the car I said to Paul, "That was our only spare." He suggested that we not have another flat. And a few miles farther down the road — we had another flat. There was no other traffic that night. What to do? A difficult situation had become dangerous. We couldn't stay in the car and keep the engine and heater running because we didn't have enough gasoline to last the night. If we elected to stay with the car, we faced the very real possibility that we would freeze to death before help came.

Paul recalled seeing a cabin about three miles back. We had no choice but to hoof it. He counseled me: "Put on all the clothing you have. Leave everything else in the car. We have to start walking and soon." He wore long underwear, I did not, though I did put on an extra pair of trousers. My long parka reached to about midthigh; from there down I could feel the biting cold. By the time we reached the cabin, I had chilblains. The kindly people who owned the cabin cautioned me, "Don't stand too close to the stove. You want to warm up slowly, otherwise the pain will be terrible. Rub your arms and legs to get the circulation going."

The family supplied us with a mound of warm blankets and fur robes. After feeding us a substantial meal of hot soup, bread and steaming coffee, they all but tucked us into beds in their cabin loft. Next morning we awakened to the aroma of frying ham and eggs and fresh-baked bread. We feasted. It wasn't until after we had finished breakfast that I thought to ask why her husband and son hadn't joined us at the meal. She explained that they had eaten long ago and gone for our car.

I protested: "How can they? It's sitting there with a flat tire and no spare." She explained that the men had taken their pickup truck to the car, removed the spare, returned to the house to patch it, and then taken it back to the car to mount it on the hub. A little later that morning the two men drove up with both vehicles.

Now — that was Alaska in those early years, that was the way people were. When I tried to pay for the night's lodging and the meals, not to mention the repair of our car, the family would take nothing.

Paul Greimann's company eventually made still another contribution to the future of Arctic Alaska Tours. Within a few years after starting Fairbanks sightseeing, the sightseeing arm of the business became more than I wanted to handle. My DeSoto and the two Chrysler limousines were too small for further increases in business. I knew that soon we must invest in larger, more costly equipment. One of Paul Greimann's top mechanics, a man named Everett Patton, came to me with the answer. He suggested that he take over the sightseeing end of the business. I agreed and he bought my three limousines and also two Beck buses to accommodate increased sightseeing needs. Patton's proposal seemed a good idea. Even though I would make little profit from the sightseeing passengers he carried, I wanted to shed the responsibility for coping with mechanical maintenance, hiring personnel, and buying new equipment. Thus, in the spring of 1951, was born Patton's Alaska Sightseeing Company.

Besides his mechanical, organizational and driving abilities, Patton had an excellent speaking voice as well as a profound knowledge of Alaska's history and lore. This knowledge added immeasurably to the interest of sightseeing tours. Years later, after the original Arctic Alaska Tours had expanded far beyond any of my reasonable hopes or unreasonable dreams, we retained Patton to train Westours' driver-guides. He is still today a consultant to Westours, spending his winters in Desert Hot Springs and summers in Alaska.

Very early in my Fairbanks sightseeing operation, I realized that a riverboat cruise would supplement and enhance the city tour that we offered by limousine. Fairbanks is situated at the confluence of the Tanana and Chena rivers, tributaries of the Yukon. These rivers are a perfect setting for a scenic tour away from the city into the Alaskan bush.

Before the airplane came to Alaska, before highways were built, before even the trails were explored, the riverways were the lifelines thrugh the North Country. For three-quarters of a century, beginning in 1869, stern-wheelers plied the Yukon River and its tributaries. By the time of the gold rush, these steamboats were a common sight all the way from St. Michael on the Bering Sea to Whitehorse in the Yukon Territory — a distance of almost 2000 miles. The stately ''antebellum'' craft brought an incongruous touch of elegance (silver and fine linen in the dining room) to the Arctic wilderness as they steamed to and from Klondike gold fields, looking for all the world like the ships you see paddlewheeling up the Mississippi in movies that depict the Old South.

The narrow-gauge White Pass & Yukon Route railroad that switchbacks across the mountains from Skagway to Whitehorse was completed in the summer of 1900. Travelers — bound for Dawson, Forty Mile, Fort Yukon, Rampart, Circle City, Eagle, Fairbanks, Nenana — would ride passenger ships from Seattle or Vancouver up the Inside Passage to Skagway where they boarded the railway to Whitehorse. From there the graceful riverboats wound their way north as far as the Arctic Circle before turning south again, to snake through the great Yukon River Valley of interior Alaska. Other rivers also knew these picturesque craft — the Kuskokwim, Innoko, Tanana.

Steamers were fueled by burning 4-foot pieces of cordwood, cut during winter months at wood camps and neatly stacked along the river. When the shallow-draft boats tied up at the bank to take on wood, passengers walked the gangplank ashore and strolled the woodcutters' trails — fringed by fireweed and burdened with the scent of wild roses. When the riverboats stopped at villages, Indians sold elaborately beaded moccasins and birch baskets to travelers. The Indians' fishwheels, placed along the riverbanks, scooped up salmon that were fileted and hung on racks to dry.

Because of the riverboats, miners could bring their families into some of the wildest and most remote parts of Alaska and the Yukon. Often — usually — the boats would push a freight-loaded barge as they moved up or down stream, winding around river bends, occasionally getting stuck on sandbars, sometimes for days at a time. The sternwheelers played an important part in Alaska transportation right up until World War II.

There was a great romantic tradition in Alaska river travel, and along about 1949 I began to search for a riverboat that would accommodate sightseers. A boat that looked promising was the *Godspeed*, owned by Bishop Gordon, a river pilot and also the Episcopal Bishop of Alaska. I approached the Bishop, explained my idea, and asked about buying or chartering his boat for excursions down the Chena into the Tanana. He was receptive to the proposal, provided I found a qualified river pilot to navigate the boat. He suggested I talk to a young man named Jim Binkley, a member of his parish and an experienced riverboat captain. Binkley operated the steam plant at the University of Alaska in Fairbanks.

The strapping young Binkley and I hit it off at once. Captivated by the idea of river excursions for visitors, he agreed to change his shift at the University steam plant so that he could pilot the boat during the day.

Bishop Gordon sold me the *Godspeed*, a 25-passenger shallow-draft vessel, ideally suited for river sightseeing tours; and from the outset, the riverboat excursions were a popular sightseeing attraction. Visitors sailed off through the Alaskan ''Outback,'' away from the city. The boat tied up (as its successor still does today) at an island in the middle of the Tanana River, allowing passengers to go ashore and walk through an Indian fish camp where they saw fish wheels, a trapper's cabin and cache, and a smokehouse.

The year following the start of these riverboat tours, Binkley became a partner in the enterprise. Later, I believe it was in 1951, I sold him the *Godspeed* and he created his own business, Alaska Riverways. He piloted the boats and took care of the passengers, leaving most of the promotion and booking chores to Arctic Alaska Tours. Eventually, Binkley built a much larger ship, the *Discovery I*, diesel-powered and patterned after the old Mississippi sternwheelers — the same kind of boat (except for its diesel engine) that sailed the Yukon during gold rush days. As Binkley's enterprise continued to grow, the *Discovery I* was followed by the even larger *Discovery II*.

Alaska Riverways is a family business. Jim and his wife Mary, and their sons and daughters have worked together to build a highly successful tourist service, which has given thousands upon thousands of visitors a memorable Alaskan experience.

Through the years, Jim Binkley established a solid reputation for honesty and stability that earned him a leading role in the Alaska tourist industry.

Expansion To
Anchorage And Seattle

Alaska Visitors Association

Many tourists, perhaps most tourists, do not understand the difference between a tour operator and a retail travel agency. *Both* sell travel — plane tickets, rail tickets, cruise berths, motorcoach transportation, hotel rooms, sightseeing, transfers. The difference is that the tour operator sells *only* "package" tours: all the pieces are "bundled" and sold as a unit. The travel agent, on the other hand, will sell you pieces *or* packages — a one-way ticket to Anchorage or an all-inclusive Alaska tour. Usually the package that you buy through a travel agency has been produced by a tour operator who creates the package and pays the agency a commission for taking care of the booking. Another difference is that most travel agents sell travel to most parts of the world, while often tour operators specialize — become experts — in certain destinations: Europe, the South Pacific, Orient, Africa, Alaska. Sometimes travel agents branch out — they become tour operators as well as travel agents and package their own tours. During our early years, Arctic Alaska Travel was *both* a retail travel agent that sold travel to all parts of the world as well as a tour operator (Arctic Alaska Tours) that specialized in Alaska.

Marguerite and I had adopted a philosophy which in today's jargon is summed up by the phrase: "Go for it!" We were always ready to "try our wings." Any misgivings we may have had, we put aside for the thrill of the adventure and the excitement of accomplishing something new and different. We were not afraid to put everything we owned in the pot. We supported each other in this. We would pledge our bank roll, our home, our life insurance — everything we had in the world — as collateral to finance a new project. We did not allow ourselves the luxury of security. Sometimes we wondered whether we would make it, but we never lost our enthusiasm for trying.

I did not pay myself a salary, but drew from the business only those funds needed to maintain my family. Our intent was not to live high on the hog, bleeding the business for whatever it would bear, but to create a tourist industry where none had existed, and to build an enduring enterprise.

I learned early that it was not necessary or even desirable to own outright every service Arctic Alaska Tours offered. By using others' experience in ground and air transport and in food preparation and innkeeping, I availed myself of their expertise and freed myself of the responsibilities for equipment purchase, maintenance, and operating staff. Arctic Alaska Tours produced a lot of income for associated firms without tying up its own capital. Examples were Jim Binkley's riverboat tours, the Wiens' taking over from me the ground services in Kotzebue, Everett Patton's purchase of my sightseeing operation in Fairbanks, and Paul Greimann's motorcoach charters.

In each case it was Arctic Alaska Tours that stimulated the need for these services and booked the business to keep them going, but in each case the services were better operated by others. In order to build something new and needed, I would form partnerships, corporations or "alliances" — and do whatever was required to make the enterprise go. I assumed full control only when a service was needed and no one else would take the initiative as in the case of my ill-fated Tent City or the more happily conceived Tanana Court Motel.

I recall again the advice of Austin "Cap" Lathrop, who had helped me locate in a proper office in Fairbanks: "Chuck, you'll be successful in business if you always take care to surround yourself with people of equal or better ability than your own." I was fortunate in having a travel agent named Betty Lee Bauer, who became my office manager and eventually headed the tour department.

A key person who joined the staff in 1948 was my long-time friend Norm Geiger. In 1948 Geiger took a summer's leave of absence from Western Airlines to come North to help me expand the business. His introduction to Arctic Alaska Tours was abrupt, to say the least. He had taken delivery of a new Chrysler limousine in California, and drove it to Alaska for use in our sightseeing program. Arriving in Fairbanks, he had no more than stepped out of the Chrysler (its front end mangled because he had struck and killed a deer) than I pounced on him, saying, "Norm, you're just in time. I have a full load of passengers for you. Without even taking time to shower and change his clothes, he stepped back in the car and began showing tourists around Fairbanks.

Geiger's three-month leave from Western Airlines extended to nearly two years. During that time he became a vice president of Arctic Alaska Travel Service.

Another key person who was to become an invaluable asset to the company was Lou West, my father, retired from the firm of West Brothers Petroleum Geologists, in which he and his brother were principals. After coming North for a visit in 1949, my parents had fallen in love with Alaska; and my father approached me about becoming our outside salesman. He wanted to help build the business and asked for the responsibility of calling on airlines and travel agents in the South 48. In years to come he became known on the West Coast, particularly in California, as *the* representative for Alaska tourism, working so enthusiastically and effectively that many in the travel industry thought Lou West, not Chuck West, owned the company he represented. He continued in this work for twenty-one years.

In 1949 we expanded our offices from Fairbanks to Anchorage. It was Cap Lathrop who suggested the office location. He owned the Fourth Avenue Theater in Anchorage, a fine building in the center of town across from the Post Office. By rearranging space in the building, Lathrop provided an excellent office with a street location. Paul Greimann's motorcoach operation shared that space with us, and Norm Geiger became our Anchorage manager. Almost from the start business was brisk — the office served as a combined retail travel agency, bus agency, and sales outlet for tours. When Geiger went back to Western Airlines (in 1951), Brad Phillips, my one-time "baggage assistant" in Fairbanks, came to Anchorage as office manager.

Not everyone in Alaska shared our enthusiasm for tourism. Restaurants and some local businesses understood the value of "new money" that tourists brought to town, and they recognized Arctic Alaska Tours as a source of increased business. On the other hand, many oldtimers resented tourists, resented being "crowded" by outsiders and the notion that cheechakos were discovering *their* Alaska. They wanted Alaska for themselves and didn't give a damn for the flow of dollars that visitors brought to the community. They did not appreciate travel for what it is, a nonpolluting source of income that exploits neither land nor water. A gold dredge rapes a river valley, leaving great ridges of ugly tailings. Tourism destroys nothing. A mountain view is forever. Tourists come by the thousands, marvel at the wilderness, shoot photographs (not wild animals), and glean memories to last a lifetime. After they depart, the scenery remains — untouched, unspoiled, ready to welcome the next group of visitors.

Curiously, even travel-related industries were sometimes opposed to tourism. Like other Alaska cities, Anchorage was not blessed with many hotels during the Forties and Fifties. Our tours used the old Parsons Hotel and the Fifth Avenue, both gone now. The two leading hotels in town, the Anchorage and the Westward, were not interested in tourist travelers. Miners, trappers, fur buyers, government people, and construction workers provided all the customers they needed. Owners of both the Westward and Anchorage hotels told me in so many words: "Don't bother us with the tourist business. If you have to do something with your tourists, at least keep them out of Anchorage. Take them out to that little hotel in Palmer (an Anchorage suburb) and keep them there."

When I observed that the tourists — and their spending money — wouldn't do Anchorage much good if sequestered in Palmer, I was told: "That's your problem, not ours. Just get them out of town."

This attitude — from the business community — was incomprehensible to me. Today, astute business people do everything in their power to lure tourists to Alaska. Over the years, this anti-tourist sentiment has disappeared. And a large part of the credit goes to the Alaska Visitors Association (the AVA).

I realized early on that if we were to counter the reactionary feelings of some of the resident oldtimers, tourism had a selling job to do. If the travel business was to flourish, we must instill in the minds of resident Alaskans the value of the "rolling tourist dollar" — the dollar that rolls from place to place, from airline to hotel to restaurant to souvenir shop, to the employees of those establishments, and to the businesses that do business with those employees.

One day in Fairbanks I talked to George Sundborg, administrative assistant to territorial governor Ernest Gruening. Sundborg agreed that we needed an organization to promote tourism. I told him the publisher of one of the travel trade publications, Robert Morgan of *Travel Agent* magazine, had offered to come to Alaska to speak about the value of tourism. Recognizing the importance of this, Sundborg offered to pay Morgan's travel expenses with funds from the territorial budget if we could assemble an influential group to hear him talk.

In short order, I invited the presidents of Wien and Northern Consolidated

Airlines and top people from other airlines in Alaska: Northwest, Pan American, Alaska Coastal, Ellis. I also approached key people with the hotels, banks, and other industries.

Morgan gave them a convincing presentation on the value of tourism to the community. From that meeting of twelve to fifteen Alaskans was born the nucleus of what is today the Alaska Visitors Association. With a modest budget, but high hopes, the fledgling assembly elected a president (banker Marshall Crutcher from Kodiak) and its first board of directors. I was one of the founding directors.

Among those most helpful in furthering government and popular support of the visitor industry were Bob Ellis of Ellis Airlines; O. F. Benecke, vice president of Alaska Coastal Airlines and later president of Alaska Airlines; A. B. "Cot" Hayes, manager of Northwest Orient Airlines in Anchorage; Raymond Peterson, president of Northern Consolidated Airlines; Jack Whaley and his brother Frank Whaley of Wien Air Alaska; Bob Rose, a vice president of Alaska Steamship Company; Frank Downey of the White Pass & Yukon Route; Helen Monsen, who owned the *Juneau Empire*; Phil Johnson, the Bank of Fairbanks; and Jim Binkley and Everett Patton.

It gives me a warm feeling of satisfaction to recall that I was instrumental in helping to create the AVA, which was to do so much to establish the value of the Alaska tourist industry. We began a campaign to promote friendliness toward visitors, who came into our great land to admire the mountains and who left mountains of tourist dollars in return without having exploited anything.

It was not so much the man-in-the-street who had been against tourism, but the city hall types and business people. Many local residents would invite tourists into their yards to show off their gardens, while commercial interests remained antagonistic: "We paid for these streets and sewers, and your damned tourists are *using* them. How do you propose we levy a 'use tax' on *them*?" That was their attitude. It took a well-planned selling job to convince minor officialdom and some of the commercial people that tourists, by patronizing local businesses, were more than paying their way — that tourists were not using resources so much as they were paying for the privilege of admiring them.

As AVA grew, branch offices were started in every major city in Alaska. These offices secured matching funds from the Territory and later from the State of Alaska. Today the organization that began with a budget of a few hundred dollars promotes Alaska with annual budgets of $7 to $8 million. From year to year, I appeared before the Alaska legislature to appeal for budget appropriations and additional support such as the formation of a State Department of Tourism.

During 1949 and '50 Arctic Alaska Tours' business continued to increase.

Its main components were still Arctic air tours, sightseeing in Anchorage and Fairbanks, and rail-bus packages that connected with Alaska Steamship Company sailings at Valdez and Seward.

As time went by, I saw ever more clearly that I must move to where my customers were, to the South 48, with Seattle as headquarters. Communication between Alaska and the outside world was not dependable: long-distance telephone connections were expensive and uncertain, Telex was not yet available, and airmail was unreliable, particularly when winter storms grounded many flights. Seattle, 1500 miles closer to my tourist markets, was the jumping-off point for ships and airplanes that carried the tourist trade to Alaska. It would be better, I decided, to "push" visitors into Alaska from Seattle than to continue to "pull" them in from Fairbanks.

In 1951 I went to Seattle looking for an opportunity to establish an office there. Harry Jarvinen, SAS manager in Seattle, approached me about being my manager. He located a one-room office on Second Avenue in the Old National Building (later "imploded" to make room for a modern skyscraper). Harry and I had established a friendship during the preceding several years. Arctic Alaska Travel Service had been a good producer for SAS, and in 1948 Marguerite and I had been his guests on an SAS inaugural flight to Scandinavia.

Earlier in this chapter, I pointed out the differences between a tour operator and a travel agent. One of the *similarities* between the two is that both require recognition from the airlines in order to receive commissions on ticket sales. To operate in Seattle our office would need airline conference appointments. We had those appointments in Anchorage and Fairbanks, but not in Seattle. At that time the airlines enforced a "need clause" which required that a new agency demonstrate a "need" for its services before the airlines would appoint it. An entrenched clique of established Seattle retail travel agents opposed my application. The main thrust of my Seattle office would be Alaska tourism, but they looked upon the new office as competition to their retail business and used their influence with the airlines to prevent my being granted the all-important airline appointments. The manager of a very large airline in Seattle told me the agents had threatened to boycott any airline that sponsored my application. None of the airlines wanted to be the first to break the impasse.

I learned that the seven or eight well-established agents who opposed my application were members of the American Society of Travel Agents (ASTA). Also a member of ASTA, I attended one of their Seattle meetings and made a speech. It wasn't a pleading, diffident speech. Now that I think back, it wasn't even a polite speech. I told them what I thought of a group of ASTA agents that banded together to boycott the application of another ASTA agent. The speech went on at some length. I ended by saying: "I'll tell you something. I'm going to be here. You might as well get used to the idea because I'm going to be in Seattle. Just get ready for it. I'm going to be here."

A few days later, Harry Jarvinen and I were driving to Vancouver, B.C., to call on Vancouver agents and Canadian Pacific Airlines about our tour programs in Alaska. We were cruising along within the legal speed limit when, a few miles south of Blaine at the Canadian-United States border, we were "howled down" by a State Highway Patrolman.

"Are you Mr. West?" the trooper asked.

Mystified, I told him I was, and he explained that a Mr. Barash in Seattle wanted me to call him from the next telephone.

Arnold Barash was owner of two Seattle travel agencies — "Where-to-Go Travel" and "University Travel." He was also the current president of the Seattle chapter of ASTA and had presided over the ASTA meeting at which I had made my "speech." Unable to imagine what had prompted his call, I stopped at the first telephone. Barash told me that he had thought over my remarks at the ASTA meeting. He said, "I believe you will do what you said you would do." He asked if I wanted to buy his travel agencies, Where-to-Go Travel and University Travel Service. He said, "I'd rather sell to you than try to oppose you." And he explained that he had been in business many years and was looking for an opportunity to retire.

I struck a deal with Barash and bought both of his travel agencies, thereby avoiding a battle with entrenched ASTA agents. By buying his agencies I acquired the needed airline appointments — I was in business in Seattle. We canceled our month-to-month lease in the Old National Building and moved into Where-to-Go Travel Service on Fourth Avenue.

From the very start, it was apparent that coming to Seattle was a good move. Our tour business took off. Seattle was — is — the gateway to Alaska. Communication with West Coast agents, our primary source of tour business, was faster, more convenient, less expensive. Alaska Steamship Company sailings originated in Seattle. So did airline flights to Alaska. Tour sales began to show strong and consistent increases each year. I realized that the future was in the tour business and not in my retail travel agencies in Fairbanks and Anchorage. In 1952 my family moved to Seattle where Marguerite and I bought a home on Magnolia Bluff, looking across Puget Sound at the Olympic Mountains.

I still had many ideas for growth and expansion. One of these was a different routing to the interior. From Haines, a few miles west of Skagway, Haines Highway follows Jack Dalton's old gold rush route across Chilkat Pass, joining the Alaska Highway at Haines Junction. Travelers could cruise north through the Inside Passage to Skagway, transfer to Haines, travel by highway to Fairbanks, then by rail to Anchorage, and return home by plane from Anchorage or by ship from Seward. But as it turned out, 1953 — when Paul Greimann and I first pursued the idea — was not the year.

Hotel rooms, scarce in Skagway, were even scarcer in Haines. Paul Greimann and I went to Haines to talk to Carl Heinmiller, one of several U.S. Army veterans who had acquired Port Chilkoot (formerly Fort William Henry Seward) from the U.S. Army in 1947. The fort's old buildings were still intact, and we talked to Heinmiller about converting two of the soldiers' barracks into a hotel. Paying Heinmiller $3,000 for a six-months' option to buy the barracks for $100,000, we hired an architect and an engineer to renovate the building. After examining the structures, both the architect and the engineer recommended against renovation: the buildings were too old; cost of refurbishing, installing partitions, lowering ceilings, rewiring, and replumbing would be too high. They recommended starting from scratch and building a new hotel. That was the end (for the time being) of the idea to run tours through Haines. A few years later the idea came to life again, and eventually at Haines I was to meet my own ships with my own buses.

During this period, I opened offices in Juneau and in Nome. Business volume supported neither, and within a short time both were closed.

Also during this period, two key people joined us who were to help guide the company's fortunes for many years:

Frank Ashida came from the University of Washington in 1951. He went into our accounting department and became a specialist in planning tour itineraries that gave us maximum utilization of facilities — motorcoaches, hotels, sightseeing. Later he also took charge of our computer department; we were one of the first tour companies to use a computer for operations as well as for accounting.

H. J. (Jack) Musiel was the top Seattle sales representative for Northwest Airlines when Harry Jarvinen hired him as sales manager for our two Seattle travel agencies. After about two years, he was lured away to become vice president of sales for a new cruise operation in San Francisco. The company had acquired one of the Alaska Steamship Company ships (renamed the *Leilani*) to sail between San Francisco and Hawaii. On the day of her first sailing — with all passengers aboard — the union struck the company and the ship never left the dock. One more American maritime venture had been killed by the unions. Meanwhile, I had decided to get out of the retail travel business and concentrate exclusively on Alaska tours. I sold the two Seattle travel agencies to Carl Helgren, later to become president of the American Society of Travel Agents, and his partner, Carl Risk. When Jack Musiel returned to Seattle about six months after he left to go to San Francisco, he became director of sales for Arctic Alaska Tours. Then when Harry Jarvinen eventually left us, Jack took over as manager of the office.

These two men, Frank Ashida and Jack Musiel, were to become mainstays in the development of Arctic Alaska Tours and its successor, Westours. Jack Musiel is today the retired chairman of the latter company. Frank Ashida is still with that company in a top executive position. Through the years, in appreciation of their services, I gave each of them shares of Westours stock, which they held until Holland America Cruises bought up all outstanding stock a few years after my departure from the company in 1973. They each received a substantial sum for their holdings, more than a million dollars between the two of them.

The Start Of "Alaska Hyway Tours"

I n 1954 Alaska Steamship Company abandoned its passenger services; and, as they say in 19th century novels, "little did I realize" the implications of this for Chuck West. On Friday, September 24, 1954, from an upstairs window of our home on Magnolia Bluff in Seattle, I watched the steamer *Denali* sail up Puget sound. It was the end of an era. Watching that ship glide past, I felt a pang of sadness, knowing that this was the last Alaska Steamship vessel to carry passengers to the Far North. But I was to learn that the pangs of nostalgia were as nothing compared to the pangs of uncertainty which that ship left in her wake.

A variety of services are woven together to form an Alaska tour: highway transportation, air transportation, cruise ships, hotel accommodations, food services, city sightseeing and transfers. The tour operator assembles these component services into "packages," which are then described in a brochure and offered for sale through retail travel agents. This prepackaging simplifies and expedites the planning of a complex tour itinerary — for *both* the retail travel agent and the traveler. Even though tours are packaged, the traveler is still offered a wide choice of itineraries.

The impasse for the Alaska tour operator during the fifties and sixties was the uncertain reliability of essential component services. Except for air transportation, which for the most part was consistently available, all other services were lacking at one or another time or place. Building an Alaska tour business was simply not possible without first building hotels, buying cruise ships, applying for motorcoach route authorities, and creating sightseeing services where none had existed. This is not the case in other parts of the world where tour companies, large and small, are able to operate without owning their own hotels, buses, cruise ships or sightseeing.

I eventually founded Westours, incorporated in 1957, because I needed

75

an umbrella company for a vast Alaska travel complex comprised of a motor-coach company (Alaska Hyway Tours), a cruise company (Alaska Cruise Lines), a sightseeing company (the Gray Line franchise for Alaska), plus three hotels (one in Fairbanks, one in Skagway, and a third at Beaver Creek in the Yukon Territory). Attempts to encourage others to establish these services did not pan out, except in a few isolated instances: for example, Jim Binkley's fine riverboat operation in Fairbanks.

The need to provide these missing pieces, which had begun with my departure from Wien Airlines in 1946, continued unabated after my move to Seattle.

With Alaska Steam out of the picture, my "Golden Belt Line" tours that connected with ships docking at Seward and Valdez would be a thing of the past. To a limited extent I was able to use the Canadian Pacific and Canadian National ships that docked at Skagway, but their space availability was not sufficient to offset the demise of Alaska Steamship Company. The change also affected Paul Greimann, who had supplied the motorcoach charters. Greimann appraised the situation, didn't like what he saw, and sold his Alaska Coachways to a man named Russ Swank, owner of a bus company called Matanuska Valley Lines.

My tour business, based on buses meeting ships, must now rely on buses meeting airplanes. Tour routes — I mistakenly thought — could be adapted to tie in with air passenger traffic instead of ship traffic. Larger aircraft were coming to Alaska. Pacific Northern, Pan American, Northwest, Alaska Star and others had introduced new planes to Alaska routes: the Lockheed Constellation, the Douglas DC-6 and DC-6B, and the Boeing Stratocruiser. Reliable bus transportation to meet these planes when they landed at Alaska airports was crucial.

In April of 1955 at the Alaska Visitors Association meeting in Juneau, I spoke with the new owner of Alaska Coachways, Russ Swank, and empha-sized the importance of his buses being in top-notch condition and ready to roll when tourists started to arrive in June. Swank told me not to worry about it: "I have the equipment and I'll be ready to take care of all the passengers you can send my way." He described the equipment and told me he had ordered several additional used, but well-maintained, buses from Gray Line in San Francisco.

Thinking over Swank's assurances I decided that the rosy picture he painted did not coincide with his past performance or with rumors I had heard of his financial difficulties. I decided I must see for myself. Accompanied by Brad Phillips, I visited Swank's garage in Anchorage where we found a yard of buses in various stages of decrepitude and disrepair — bodies dented, frames bent, windows broken, wheels and axles lying on the ground. Months would be needed to put them in shape.

One of Swank's mechanics was there. I asked him about the bus carcasses scattered about; my heart sank when he told me, "They're deadline. Those I gotta get ready for the summer tourist trade." I knew that no way in the world could Swank's people restore those buses in time for the summer rush of business.

Recalling that Swank had mentioned buying used buses from Gray Line, I telephoned Gray Line's San Francisco office and inquired about the buses they were preparing for delivery to Russ Swank in Alaska.

"Swank?? Who's he??" was the response.

For an instant — it seemed — my sunken heart actually stopped beating. This was April. My tourists would begin to arrive in early June little more than a month away; and the buses to carry them were nowhere in sight.

Questioning further, I learned that although Swank had ordered no buses, Gray Line did have buses for sale; I boarded a plane for San Francisco. There, I came to quick agreement with Gray Line's manager of surplus equipment and bought four used Flxible buses that I loaded with spare parts — extra wheels, drive shafts, springs. My next stop was an automotive body shop where the buses were painted blue and gold.

While this was being done, I scouted around, found four local firemen on vacation, hired them as drivers and set off leading a four-bus caravan to Seattle. There, I paused only long enough to change clothes and pick up my young son Charles to accompany me on the long, difficult drive North.

Spring "breakup" is the worst season of the year to drive the Alaska Highway. We coped with mud, floods, landslides and every imaginable kind of weather. From Seattle our blue-and-gold procession drove north to the Canadian border. We passed through the Fraser River Canyon to interior British Columbia, then turned north again through the Cariboo Country to Prince George in central British Columbia, then north and east to Dawson Creek, beginning point of the Alaska Highway, then northwest via Dawson Creek, Fort St. John, Fort Nelson, Watson Lake and Whitehorse to Tok in Alaska. Total distance from San Francisco was more than 3,000 miles. But we made it.

Those firemen were hardy, strong, hard working, personable, macho guys — experienced at handling heavy equipment. They looked upon the trek north as a great lark and were eager to make the adventure a success. But at one point we encountered a problem that none of us could handle. As we approached Prince George in central British Columbia, a bus broke a bell housing in heavy highway mud. Using one of the other buses we managed to tow it into Prince George where we discovered (on Saturday) that the only garage in town was closed. The owner's name was on the door. I called him at home and explained our situation: if we waited until Monday to begin repairing the bus we would lose a full day. And every day was precious. The owner gave me the name of his mechanic and told me that it would be all right if the mechanic worked in the garage on his own time provided I paid him double time for his weekend work. That was fine by me.

The mechanic was a twenty-four-year-old German man, who turned out to be perhaps the finest mechanic I have ever known. As part of his apprentice training in Germany, he had built an engine *from scratch*, including the casting of his own parts. He was a master. And he fixed our bus. We rolled out of Prince George the following day, Sunday, and by nightfall were one hundred miles up the road.

When we arrived in Tok at the intersection of the Alaska and Glenn highways, I telephoned Brad Phillips in Anchorage, told him about the buses, asked him to meet two of them in Palmer (near Anchorage) and put them in temporary storage. Then I drove on to Fairbanks, where I parked the other two buses on the lot at the Tanana Court and called Paul Greimann. I explained to Greimann that Swank had misrepresented his ability to perform, and I asked him to repossess Alaska Coachways and to buy or lease from me the four Gray Line buses needed for the summer season. Greimann agreed, in principle, but learned when he met with his attorney and Swank's accountants that Swank's company was in miserable financial shape and not worth repossessing. Liabilities exceeded assets substantially; repossession would mean throwing good money after bad. Greimann had lost everything — his motorcoach company and the money he had expected to receive for it.

Then he reminded me that his deal with Swank had included selling the authority to operate buses on Alaska highways. Neither he nor I could carry bus passengers without the blessing of the Alaska Transportation Commission (ATC). Greimann believed the commission would act too slowly for us to operate that season; he suggested that I make an accommodation with Swank. I preferred to do battle with the ATC and flew to Juneau where I was able to petition an extraordinary session of the transportation commission, made up of the lieutenant governor, attorney-general and state auditor. Explaining the situation to them, I asked for temporary authority to form a company called Alaska Hyway Tours. The three-man commission heard my story and recognized the detrimental impact Swank's failure to perform would have on the Alaskan tourist industry. They granted my request.

Swank was so furious when he discovered what had transpired at state offices in Juneau that he served an injunction on my new bus operation. By now *I* was furious. I decided I would fly my passengers before I would yield to Swank. The immediate problem was to transport them between Whitehorse and Fairbanks. Tour passengers would arrive on CPR and CNR ships at Skagway, take the train to Whitehorse, transfer there to British Yukon Navigation Company (BYN) buses for the trip on the Alaska

Highway to the border where they were to be met by Swank's buses for transportation to Fairbanks. I had planned — after Alaska Hyway Tours received its authority — to operate the same service to connect with the same company, BYN. I had informed Frank Downey of the White Pass & Yukon (which owned BYN) of this, and he had agreed to provide the connecting service.

Now, Swank's injunction prevented my operation between Fairbanks and the border. Rather than allow Swank to carry passengers that I had sold, I decided to charter airplanes and fly my people between Whitehorse and Fairbanks — and so informed Frank Downey who agreed to redirect my customers to the airport at Whitehorse. For a period of several days we flew them by charter. Swank's buses ran down to the border empty and returned empty because there weren't any passengers there. The injunction was temporary and the charter arrangement was soon lifted.

This series of unanticipated crises had catapulted me into the bus business. In order to incorporate Alaska Hyway Tours I needed incorporators besides myself and I asked four men to come in with me: Everett Patton, Brad Phillips, Jim Binkley, and Jack Whaley of Wien Air. They didn't put up a lot of money but were happy to be a part of the venture. I asked Patton to exchange his Alaska Sightseeing Company stock for stock in Alaska Hyway Tours. Each of the other men put in $1,000 each. My investment was the $20,000 I had spent for the buses, which gave me majority control. Everett Patton was the company's first president. Two years later, in 1957, when Westours was formed and Alaska Hyway Tours became a part of that company, the four incorporators exchanged their Alaska Hyway Tours stock for Westours stock. Westours' Alaska Hyway Tours division remains to this day the largest motorcoach operation in Alaska.

The four buses we used to start the company — that arrived in the nick of time to get us through a crisis at the beginning of our 1955 season — served us for ten seasons, carried thousands of passengers, and were eventually replaced by newer equipment. In September of 1984 I was in Skagway and happened to notice two of those original four coaches rusting away in a cow pasture — still recognizable in their blue and gold colors. I suggested to Westours that one of them be restored and placed in a museum — museums restore historic old trains, why not buses?

Travel by motorcoach is a far better way to tour Alaska than travel by plane. Tourists want to ride *through* the wilderness, not look down on it from 30,000 feet. Nothing delights a group of passengers more than to sit in a bus and wait for a moose to mosey off the road. That's when the cameras start to click.

Luckily, none of my drivers ever hit a large animal, although automobiles on Alaska highways regularly kill or maim wild creatures. These unfortunate occurrences are frequently unavoidable; so were other hazards during those early days before the highways were improved. An earth slide once nearly carried one of our buses off the road. Another time a great boulder came tumbling down the mountain and struck a bus "amidships." In neither instance were passengers injured.

With my new motorcoach company operating, I thought that I had weathered the crisis created when Alaska Steamship Company stopped carrying passengers. But during the next two tourist seasons I was to learn that motorcoach problems had been just the beginning. In 1954, the last year of Alaska Steam operation, I sold 2,200 tours. In 1955, I sold 1,200 tours. By 1956, still with no ships operating, I sold just 800 tours.

I had to do something — and quickly — if my still-young enterprise was to be saved.

The Start of "Alaska Cruise Lines"

With tour sales diminishing each year because of Alaska Steam's withdrawal from passenger service, I realized that I had underestimated the importance of the Inside Passage as an Alaska tour component. This fabulous cruise route is unmatched anywhere in the world: 1,000 miles of tidewater wilderness, tranquil natural waterways protected from the open sea, a tapestry of islands and islets crowned with conifers and cut off from the rest of the world by an unbroken backdrop of alpine peaks.

Cruise travelers on the Inside Passage, unlike cruise travelers in other parts of the world, are not preoccupied mainly with social activities: night club entertainment, deck sports, bridge games, the bar. Their main activity is roaming the deck or sitting in a lounge chair and watching the wilderness go by — spotting eagles, whales, porpoise. Some of the narrow, glacier-carved channels — first explored in the 18th Century by Spanish, English and Russian sailing ships — resemble rivers more than arms of the sea. Travelers view an ever-changing panorama of forests, islands, mountains, glaciers.

It's sublime. And in some places it's more sublime than in others. Glacier Bay, fifty miles long, is surrounded by mammoth glaciers which descend from surrounding mountains to form towering cliffs of ice that break off and thunder into the sea. In Tracy Arm Fjord waterfalls hundreds of feet high streak down sheer granite cliffs into ice-mantled waters. At the head of the fjord, deep in the mountains, glaciers press down to the water's edge, breaking off into huge chunks of ice to become floating rest stops for seal and waterfowl.

Ports of call along the Inside Passage would be mere hamlets in more populous parts of the world, yet each has its special interest: Ketchikan's salmon industry and Indian totems, Sitka's Russian history, Juneau's

Mendenhall Glacier and state museums, Skagway's gold rush memories, Haines' mountain scenery.

My previous tour patterns had centered farther north. I had taken the Inside Passage for granted. Many of my customers had been a spillover of travelers who had bought a cruise from Alaska Steam and then decided to see more of Alaska almost as an afterthought. Now, with the cruise element missing, my tour business was in trouble.

I had already established a pattern for resolving such problems. When I needed sightseeing services I bought a "for hire" license and the DeSoto Suburban. When I needed a hotel I built the Tanana Court. When no one else would operate a satisfactory bus service I started Alaska Hyway Tours. Now, I needed a ship for the Inside Passage cruise: the principle was the same, but the investment was significantly greater.

At that time, other ship companies besides Alaska Steam operated between Vancouver, B.C., and Skagway, including Canadian National and Canadian Pacific; however, none of the other companies would allot sufficient space to accommodate our tour requirements. Scouting around, I was able to find a solution.

Union Steamships, Ltd., founded in 1889, ran freight and passenger services to remote logging and fishing districts of British Columbia and Alaska. Following World War II, the company converted three British Castle-class corvettes (small warships) into passenger-cargo ships for its Alaska run to Skagway. I learned the company had not been successful in keeping these passenger ships filled, so I approached them with the idea of my chartering one of the ships — the *Coquitlam* — during the 1957 summer season. Union Steam was agreeable.

That summer we sold 2,500 passengers an Inside Passage cruise as part of an Alaska cruise-tour package. We sold nearly every available berth.

We did not attempt to sail the small converted corvette, renamed the Glacier Queen, across the sometimes-rough Gulf of Alaska to Seward and Valdez. Instead, we adopted several tour variations that connected with the ship in Skagway at the northern end of the Inside Passage. Disembarking passengers rode the White Pass & Yukon Route narrow-gauge railway across the Coast Mountains to Whitehorse where they boarded motorcoaches to travel the Alaska Highway to Fairbanks. Another popular tour followed a "horseshoe" route — Skagway-Whitehorse-Haines. We called this the "Golden Horseshoe." The hotel shortage in Haines had been solved when the former officers' quarters at Port Chilkoot (Fort William Henry Seward) was converted into the Halsingland Hotel.

During the great Klondike Gold Rush of 1898, two slender trails provided the only access from coastal Alaska across the mountains to the Yukon. One was the Chilkoot Trail from Dyea near Skagway to the headwaters of the Yukon River at Lake Bennett. The other was the Dalton Trail from Haines across Chilkat Pass. Each route became a legend, and not because of the scenery, which held little interest in 1898. Only the lure of gold could entice men across that wild jumble of peaks and ridges. Alaska was settled because of gold, not scenery.

The gold is gone now, most of it. Scenery remains — along with legends, tall tales, and history. In 1957 when we began cruise service on the Inside Passage, a highway followed the Chilkat Trail to the interior; and a railroad crossed White Pass, paralleling the Chilkoot Trail.

The narrow-gauge White Pass & Yukon Route railway, completed in July, 1900, looks down on historic Gold Rush scenes, climbs nearly 3,000 feet in its first twenty miles, switchbacks up heavily forested ridges, hugs sheer mountain sides, and offers sweeping views of primitive mountain scenery and of Skagway far below. Crossing the summit of White Pass, the railroad winds through rocky, broken country that looks as though the ice age had departed only weeks ago.

The train stopped at Lake Bennett for a "Gold Rush" luncheon. Hungry travelers piled off and into a big warehouse-like dining room for a meal of beef (moose meat, in Gold Rush days), potatoes, gravy, steaming vegetables, pie.

It was at Lake Bennett that Klondike stampeders wintered in 1897-98, as they deforested the surrounding hillsides to build crude boats and rafts which, when the ice thawed that spring, carried them down the Yukon to Whitehorse. The log church they built still stands on a knoll overlooking the lake.

Constructed to supply the Klondike, the railroad soon — very early in the century — drew sightseeing travelers on one-day or overnight excursions from Skagway. Some of these travelers boarded the Yukon riverboats at Whitehorse and sailed off hundreds of miles into the Northern bush.

In 1978 a White Pass highway was opened. Competition from the highway, combined with the decline in ore shipments from the interior and excessive union demands upon the White Pass & Yukon Route, eventually forced the railroad out of business. A part of its service, the scenic trip for tourists from Skagway into the mountains, was reinstated in 1988.

When, after the war, the Alaska Highway replaced the Yukon River as a transportation artery, travelers had to substitute a ship-rail-bus connection if they wanted to explore the interior. Arctic Alaska Tours' contribution was to "package" this ship-rail-bus tour and to provide — in the same package — hotels, transfers, and city sightseeing.

During that summer season of 1957, when I discovered that our new tour patterns were successful and that we could operate the *Glacier Queen* at a profit, I told Union Steam that I wanted to buy the chartered ship — and another just like her. I didn't have the capital to buy two ocean-going passenger ships, but it was one of those times when I was so sure that I was making the right move that I put my home, my life insurance, my entire net worth on the line. And though some people thought I was crazy, my philosophy was — is — if you don't take risks, you can't expect to win — at anything. I had no alternative if I was to pursue my dream. Because Alaska Steam had dropped its passenger business, I had to find another way to get my tourists to Alaska — by ship, not by air. I needed those corvettes.

Even with everything I owned in the kitty, I still didn't have enough to underwrite the financing of both ships. I began a search for investors or guarantors and invited a group of Alaska and Seattle bankers, publishers, and other leading lights as my guests on an Inside Passage cruise. I asked them to consider helping me finance the two ships. Only one of the group, Ben Crawford, offered any support at all. He said he would loan me $25,000 — not nearly enough.

So I went to the White Pass and Yukon Route and explained the kind of revenue I would generate for their transportation system. WP&Y management had already seen the amount of business generated by the first ship and agreed to guarantee up to $500,000 on my note to finance the two 1,800-ton, 257-foot vessels. It was a good proposition for me because the WP&Y guarantee allowed me to retain ownership of the ships without my putting up equity. It was also a good proposition for the WP&Y, because I fed passengers to both ends of their rail and bus service: my ships met their train at Skagway, my buses met their buses at the Alaska-Yukon border. Their services were right in the middle; they earned revenue with every tour passenger I sold.

Thus began "Alaska Cruise Lines." We renamed the second ship the *Yukon Star* and painted it and the *Glacier Queen* blue-and-gold, the same colors that were used by our motorcoach division, Alaska Hyway Tours. For our cruise logo we used a white polar bear in a blue triangle, which appeared on ensigns, officers' caps, the ships' stacks, and on all the line's publications, menus, and promotional materials.

We installed cocktail lounges in the forward part of each ship (formerly the purser's quarters). Shuffleboard courts were painted on the top decks. My wife Marguerite supervised the addition of many of the amenities that transformed a one-time warship into a comfortable cruise liner. Cabins were repainted and spruced up with colorful draperies and bedspreads. On-board entertainment included movies, bingo, costume nights, captain's dinners and all manner of activities to entertain our passengers — when they weren't strolling the deck, leaning on the rail, or sitting in a lounge chair watching the scenery go by.

Ports of call were Prince Rupert, Ketchikan, Petersburg, Juneau, Haines and Skagway. Passengers disembarked at each port to shop, walk around town, or join sightseeing tours. Later the ships added a call at Sitka. We also cruised in Glacier Bay National Monument and Tracy Arm Fjord. Shuttling vessels passed one another midway on their regular four-day-up, four-day-back schedule between Vancouver and Skagway.

Much of the credit for the successful cruise operation goes to the Canadian crews we were able to retain when we purchased the ships from Union Steamship. One of our senior captains was also a Canadian, Ernest Shepherd of the *Yukon Star*; the other was a Scotsman, William McCombe. The two were as far apart, temperamentally, as any two men could be. Captain Shepherd was every inch the gentlemanly, polished master mariner. He got his ship under way and brought her into port using no more than hand signals and softly spoken commands. Yet every signal he gave and every command he spoke received an instant response from his crew.

On the other hand, Captain McCombe could be heard from one end of the dock to the other and for several docks in each direction, as he bellowed commands through a bullhorn or over the ship's public address system. His choice of words when calling attention to a crew member's lapse into error was more fitting to a Bering Sea whaling ship than a passenger cruise liner. McCombe's rough language sent many a woman passenger scuttling to her cabin, ears aflame, unable to believe she had heard the words that had just blistered the air. Captain McCombe's style in handling a vessel matched his language. Sometimes I wondered if he thought of his ship as a battering ram. Many a pier was nicked, splintered or adjusted from plumb as he brought the ship alongside. But all in all he was a fine skipper. We came to rely on his can-do spirit to get the job done. And I think his colorful personality and language were what many passengers expected from the North.

During thirteen years operating those ships, we never suffered an injury to a passenger. To be sure, we scuffed a few docks and experienced other minor mishaps, but nothing that could be called disastrous. Once when the *Glacier Queen* was departing Vancouver, the skipper rang down to the engine room for "slow astern." A third-engineer below decks misunderstood the bell signal and gave the captain "slow ahead." Two thousand tons of forward motion were stopped by a cold storage freezing plant filled with frozen salmon, instantly converting the *Glacier Queen* into a fish boat as she rammed the dock, smashed floor supports of the freezer plant, and caused thousands of pounds of frozen salmon to cascade down on her decks. Departure was delayed while the fish were off-loaded onto the docks and decks hosed down.

Another time, in the Strait of Georgia near Vancouver, the pilot of a Japanese freighter misread his radar one night and turned port instead of starboard, causing the freighter to ram the bow section of the *Glacier Queen*. We made it back safely to Vancouver but missed two sailings while the damage was repaired. And once a ship touched bottom in Wrangell Narrows but did not go hard aground.

On still another occasion, in Tracy Arm Fjord an eddy caught the *Yukon Star*, throwing her against a huge iceberg. Just moments before, a woman in one of the staterooms had ordered a bucket of ice to be brought to her cabin. When the ship brushed the iceberg, air scoops alongside the porthole of her cabin scraped the "berg" and showered shaved ice into her cabin to a depth of about three feet. Later she was to say to other passengers, "I ordered ice, all right — but *that* was ridiculous."

All our cooks were Chinese. They did an excellent job but spoke little English, keeping largely to themselves and not mixing with the rest of the crew. The chief cook controlled the entire galley operation, down to paying his own, well-disciplined crew, who seldom went ashore and spent their time playing cards in their quarters or sometimes fishing over the side. They were quiet, dependable people.

Once in Glacier Bay National Monument an incident involved these Chinese galley people. It was our practice when passing Bartlett Cove to pick up a Forest Service representative, who came aboard to deliver a natural history narration for the passengers. In those days, regulations against fouling the water were not nearly as strict as they are today. Ships' crews could get away with dumping garbage into the sea — *but not in Glacier Bay* where nothing, but nothing, was to go over the side into those pristine waters.

The Chinese worked below decks and seldom knew exactly where we were. On this particular day, just as the cutter bearing the Forest Service representative was coming alongside, one of the Chinese galley crew sloshed a large garbage pail of swill into the scuppers which carried the waste over the side. His timing could never have been worse — nor his aim better. The whole mess splattered down on the deck of the cutter, bespattering the very officer who was coming aboard to talk to our passengers. We were in deep trouble — $5,000 worth of trouble! In a court hearing, the fine was reduced to $1,000; even the Forest Service officer saw the humor in the situation. On future sailings, we made it a point to inform our galley crew when we entered restricted waters. We also stipulated that **they** would pick up the tab for the next violation. They may not have understood English, but they understood *that*.

Today, ships are required to contain all their sewage and garbage for disposal at designated stations ashore. Alaskan waters benefit immensely from this ruling.

Food on board was "North American," excellently prepared but not "fancy": hearty soups, beef and pork roasts, short ribs with gravy and browned potatoes — that kind of thing. A typical dessert would have been a generous slice of apple pie served with cheddar cheese. At dinners we often served a fish course, cod or halibut, as a starter and then went on to the main meal. Our galley baked all our own breads and pastries, and used a lot of butter in recipes. The cooks liked to prepare Chinese food for the passengers. Often they would cook up a late-night Chinese supper, open to anyone who wanted a midnight snack. Whatever the meal, we served plenty of good food — passengers dined often and well.

Traditionally, ships in the Alaska trade had lain over thirty-six hours in Skagway, allowing passengers time to ride the train across White Pass to Carcross where they boarded a sternwheeler steamer for an excursion to Ben-my-Chree at the end of Tagish Lake. And though the rail and lake trip was delightful and very popular, ships were idle during the thirty-six hours required for the inland excursion. They were also idle for twenty-four hours in Vancouver, the southern turnaround, to give crews a "rest up" layover that was felt to be necessary. Alaska Cruise Lines changed that policy. Our ships made the turnaround at each end in twelve hours, thereby cutting the total round-trip tie-up time from sixty to twenty-four hours. Since most of our customers were tour passengers, they traveled the Skagway-Bennett-Whitehorse rail trip as part of their tour package and then continued on to Fairbanks.

Crews didn't like the change; creditors of Alaska Cruise Lines thought it was marvelous. Ships (also buses and planes) must be kept moving if they are to pay their way. And keep them moving we did, even though it meant that engineers, electricians and welders sometimes worked while ships were underway. Meanwhile, the line paid its bills.

Another decision that helped increase revenue was to extend the Alaska travel season by adding one or two sailings at the beginning and end of the traditional season. By lengthening the cruise schedule a little more each year, we established the only five-month cruise season in the history of Alaska. We did this by offering a twenty-five percent discount to cruise passengers in May and September, and by publishing rainfall and hours-of-sunshine charts for the shoulder seasons. We adopted the slogan, "May days are Alaska's sunny days."

During our thirteen years of carrying passengers, we maintained a 97.5 percent occupancy rate, the highest load factor average in the history of Inside Passage cruising. Each of these elements — the faster turnaround, the longer seasons, and the high occupancy rate — helped us pay the debt for the ships in about five years. We gave the traveling public a product they wanted, and the public responded.

The Alaska Highway

During Arctic Alaska Tours' first eleven years (1946 to 1956), our tour patterns focused on the great expanse of wilderness between Fairbanks and Anchorage — the Alaska Range, Chugach Range, Mt. McKinley National Park, Alaska Railroad and Richardson Highway. In 1957, with the formation of Alaska Cruise Lines and Westours, we were suddenly operating in an entirely different region — the Inside Passage. And though both regions are in Alaska, they are six hundred miles apart. We needed to transport our passengers between the two — from Whitehorse (one hundred ten miles from Skagway at the northern end of the Inside Passage) to Fairbanks (one hundred miles south of the Arctic Circle). The link was the Alaska Highway.

Constructed as a wartime supply route during World War II, the Alaska Highway runs from Dawson Creek in northern British Columbia to Fairbanks in central Alaska, total distance 1,520 miles. Built in just eight months between March and November of 1942, it is one of the remarkable road-building feats of all time.

From Whitehorse the highway goes west and north past Lake Kluane, Kluane National Park, and the incredibly rugged St. Elias Mountains. It crosses the Alaska-Yukon Border at Beaver Creek and then follows the great Tanana River Valley of interior Alaska to Fairbanks.

As I mentioned before, our motorcoach division, Alaska Hyway Tours, did not have authority to serve Yukon communities. Bus service within the Yukon Territory was provided by British-Yukon Navigation Company, a subsidiary of the White Pass & Yukon Route railway. Our Alaska Hyway Tours buses met British-Yukon buses at the border where passengers transferred from one bus to the other.

Eventually, Westours developed motorcoach tour packages that traveled by highway all the way from Seattle to Fairbanks. At first, however, we used only the six-hundred-mile Whitehorse-Fairbanks segment. And six hundred miles is too far to travel in one day — on a motorcoach. This meant that we must resolve yet another hotel problem: we needed overnight accommodations midway between Whitehorse and Fairbanks. Lodging must be comfortable, clean, dependable, and also provide good restaurant facilities, a tall order in that remote part of the world.

Until about 1959, I was able to make do with existing accommodations along the highway, but then the size of our busloads began to outgrow the number of rooms available at any single accommodation. At Scottie Creek, Alaska, near the Alaska-Yukon border was an old roadhouse, built to accommodate Alaska Highway construction workers during the war. The owners, Fred Lappi and his wife Betty, had converted the roadhouse into a lodge, which we used for nearly two years. But there were problems at Scottie Creek: we needed more space than Lappi could provide and the water was not potable. Lappi hauled in all his water for drinking and cooking, not a good recommendation for a lodge and restaurant. I began to search for an alternative.

A few miles away at Beaver Creek on the Canadian side of the border, a man named Clyde Wann and his wife, Helen, had built (in 1955) a lodge with about ten rooms and a restaurant. Good water flowed from their well and they maintained a small garage and a gas pump — a convenience for our drivers. Moreover, their location was across the street from the Canadian Customs House — a convenience for our passengers. Wann appeared to be a good manager; his wife was a fine cook. With expansion, the Beaver Creek facility would meet our needs for highway accommodations.

When I approached Wann about erecting another building to give us more rooms, his reply was, "Nope, wouldn't want to do that. We like this place fine as it is." I explained that his ten rooms would not accommodate a busload of travelers; we must have more rooms. He conceded that he would like to have more business but would not agree to put up another building: "We like it just fine as it is." I told him I would guarantee him the customers needed to fill a new addition. His response to that reassurance was, "We like it just fine as it is."

So I went back to Fred Lappi at Scottie Creek. He knew of property with a good view of the mountains at Deadman Lake. He said he would build a lodge there if I would support it. I suggested he stake it out but not begin construction until I was sure what I wanted to do — his proposal entailed a delay, and the location at Beaver Creek was more convenient.

I went back to see Wann, this time accompanied by Everett Patton, the man who had bought my Fairbanks sightseeing operation. Wann's restaurant was so filled with customers there was no space to hold a conversation, so the limousine Patton and I were driving became our meeting room. When

Wann restated his determination *not* to expand his lodge, I suggested that he sell out to me and let *me* build the expansion. He was noncommittal. I explained that if I didn't build in Beaver Creek, I would have to build on the Alaska side of the border and would be competing with him instead of bringing him business. He said, "You wouldn't want to pay what I'd be asking." I inquired how much that was. He gave me a figure and I agreed to it. We named the facility "Alas/kon Border Lodge," built the needed additional rooms, and through the years, as Westours' business grew, continued to expand it. Today the handsome log structure accommodates more than three hundred overnight guests.

Besides overnight accommodations at Beaver Creek, we also found good luncheon stops along the road. Our highway travelers enjoyed substantial and wholesome meals in isolated roadside restaurants adorned by mooseracks over the fireplace and often colorful cotton curtains on the windows. Restaurants offered roasts, stews or chops — typically served with wild cranberries or blueberries. Menus often included fresh trout or pike as well as fresh salads and vegetables (most of the lodges had their own gardens). After a meal like that, topped off with a large slab of home-made pie and a cup of steaming coffee, our customers reboarded the bus in a happy frame of mind — prepared to view still more of the northern wilderness.

On their 1,700-mile journey from Vancouver to Fairbanks, travelers followed an interesting, varied, and beautiful route — first the Inside Passage cruise to Skagway, then the narrow-gauge railroad across the mountains to Whitehorse, then the Alaska Highway through the sub-Arctic interior to Fairbanks. This ship-rail-motorcoach "corridor" became the lifeline of Alaska tourism; a sea-and-land route to the northern Alaska interior, replete with magnificent wilderness scenery and the excitement of the northern frontier.

The large majority of Alaska visitors still travel that same 1,700-mile "corridor" to Fairbanks. And though changes and variations have been introduced through the years, the basic pattern remains the same. The "classic" Alaska tour (known for years at Westours as "Tour 4") was a fourteen-day package that followed the 1700-mile "corridor" to Fairbanks and then rode the Alaska Railroad south to McKinley National Park and Anchorage where travelers connected to Seattle by air. The tour was available in either direction — cruise north, fly south, or vice versa. Since the completion in 1970 of the George Parks Highway linking Anchorage-McKinley-Fairbanks, travelers have had the option of using either highway or rail for that part of the tour.

One change, a sad change, was the 1983 discontinuance of service by the White Pass & Yukon Route railway. Basic tour patterns continued as before except for substitution of highway instead of rail travel from Skagway to Whitehorse. The railroad route was partially resurrected in 1988.

I believe that it was in in 1968 that we first introduced motorcoach tours from Seattle all the way to Alaska by highway. The preceding autumn I accompanied Howard Hansen and several members of the sales staff on a trip down the highway from Fairbanks to Beaver Creek and Haines. This was the same Howard Hansen who many years earlier had sat on the back seat of a crippled Beck bus and held the carburetor in place while the bus made its way over the Richardson Highway to Fairbanks. He and I traveled together through the North Country on many different projects.

On that autumn trip with the sales staff, we stopped to look at Alas/kon Border Lodge and I asked Howard what he thought of it. He told me we should add another section: "We could sure use the rooms." That sounded good. So we did it. A new wing with forty rooms was ready for visitors when the tourist season opened the following spring.

It was on this trip that I decided to explore expansion of our motorcoach itineraries to include a highway tour from Seattle to Alaska. As we continued our trip from Beaver Creek down to Haines it occurred to me that the busy-ness of the summer season was finished and *right now* would be a good time to drive the highway to Seattle and make notes of the hotels and lodges we might use. I asked Howard to take a Chevrolet van that we kept at Haines and drive to Seattle on an exploratory trip, checking out hotels and restaurant facilities.

He protested, "I've never even been down the highway before."

I assured him that it would be a new and interesting experience for him. And it was. He dealt with rain, sleet, mud and snow — and a flying rock that punched a hole in the Chevrolet muffler. But he had a good eye for restaurants and roadside accommodations; Westours continued for many years to use facilities that Howard selected on that first trip.

Through the years, miscellaneous adventures kept us busy and entertained as we continued to add new "pieces" to the company.

In about 1962 I began negotiations with the Bank of California in Seattle to finance building the Fairbanks Inn, a modern concrete and steel hotel, in place of the old wooden-frame Tanana Court. Total investment would be more than $1 million. I left the Bank of California with the understanding that I was to invest the first $300,000 in the foundation and subfloor, and when that work was done the bank would finance completion of the building. With this understanding, I spent my equity money on the initial construction and then returned to the bank for the remainder of the financing. At that point the bank reneged and would not fulfill its commitment. I was aghast. At no time had there been any indication that the bank would back out of our agreement. There I was with $300,000 spent in initial construction and contracts signed for completion of the hotel.

I walked out of the Bank of California offices and across the street to Pacific National Bank where they were delighted to have my business. Thus was born a banking relationship that has endured to this day. Had I not found another bank to lend me the money, I would have been in serious financial difficulty — not ruined quite — but uncomfortable certainly for a while. The concrete and steel addition was completed in 1964. I learned later that the bank had other customers, competitors of mine, who had apparently influenced the bank's withdrawal of support for my Fairbanks hotel. In my opinion this was an unethical act. I was — and am — reminded of a line from an old "Maverick" television show: "If you can't trust your banker, who can you trust?"

We also built a hotel in Skagway, the Klondike Inn. With more and more cruise-tour passengers passing through Skagway, I needed control over room availabilities there. At one time, I thought that I had bought the Golden North Hotel, built in 1898. I had signed an earnest money agreement with Myrtle Lee, owner of the hotel, and had drawn up a contract to buy it. This was in the winter of 1965-66. Then I learned that she had cancelled our agreement because Norm Kneisel of Green Carpet Tours in Portland offered her more money. I considered going to court, but courts move slowly and our tourists would begin to arrive in Skagway the following May. Instead, I started to build — in midwinter — another hotel, the Klondike Inn. Ken Friske, manager of the Fairbanks Inn, supervised this construction during the long, cold winter. We dynamited the ground and built the hotel beneath the shelter of an enormous plastic tent. Forty rooms were ready for occupancy when the tourist season started that spring. That's how Westours acquired the Klondike Inn.

Not all my decisions were good ones. Tent City in Fairbanks had been my most disastrous misadventure but not the only one. Another miscalculation involved Captain Otis Triber, who had built a 65-foot yacht, the *Sea Otter*, with accommodations for sixteen passengers. The Captain proposed that we promote a luxury cruise tour for monied travelers who wanted something different — like a month-long cruise exploring out-of-the-way channels, bays and coves along the Inside Passage — Taku Inlet, Princess Louisa Inlet, Icy Stait, Tracy Arm, and others.

This sounded like a good idea and I went for it — with modifications. I was concerned that travelers would feel confined living a month at a time aboard a sixty-five foot vessel. I reached a compromise with Captain Triber, and we packaged a tour that combined a shorter yacht cruise with a land tour via Cadillac limousine purchased especially for this project. Then we promoted the tour — and the damn thing didn't sell. In spite of Otis Triber's enthusiasm and intimate knowledge of Alaskan waters, we were never able to sell more than eight or ten passengers per sailing aboard his beautiful little yacht. Triber eventually took the *Sea Otter* to Florida and the Bahamas. And I was left with a Cadillac limousine I didn't need.

Usually though, I was a pretty good promoter. From the time that I first began the Arctic coast excursions to Nome and Kotzebue, I had been able to package and sell Alaska tours. My initial single sheet flyers evolved into large color brochures, slide shows and motion picture productions. We held seminars, luncheons, dinners and other entertainments for travel agents in California and other parts of the country. I attended these, wearing an Alaskan fur-cowled parka. Eskimos sometimes accompanied us and performed their songs and story dances.

Once in Hollywood we staged an old-time "Alaska Night" and invited travel agent guests to come in pioneer costumes. We served dinner in a banquet hall at the Roosevelt Hotel decorated in Alaskan motif. And we gave out Alaskan souvenirs. Another time we took a whole troupe of Eskimos to the national ASTA convention in San Francisco. And to the international ASTA convention in Honolulu we took a honky-tonk piano player and can-can dancers. Our guys were dressed in straw hats and garter arm bands. At our private bar in the "Sourdough Suite" of the Royal Hawaiian Hotel, we served "Moose Milk" cocktails — whiskey and milk — by the gallon, literally.

We Need A Third Ship

Those were golden years. The company ran smoothly and profitably and continued to grow. I had fought my way through, made the right decisons, found the right people for key positions. I owned hotels, a fleet of modern motorcoaches, cruise ships — the works. I was building a travel empire. My family lived in a beautiful home overlooking Puget Sound. And I was enjoying it.

One of my thrills was owning a V-35 Beechcraft Bonanza, which I flew to Alaska on regular inspection trips of our properties and services. I would fly over our ships underway in the Inside Passage, then land at Skagway to inspect the Klondike Inn, then continue on to Alas/kon Boarder Lodge at Beaver Creek, and then to Fairbanks to check out the Fairbanks Inn and the motorcoach operation. From the air I was able to observe the entire operation of Westours — with, I confess, a great sense of pride in the burgeoning and successful company I had built. During this period I first heard the sobriquet "Mr. Alaska" from people in the Alaska travel industry. There was little in the Alaska tourist industry that I had not developed or influenced.

But under the surface trouble was forming. And I didn't see it. I had become accustomed to *making* things work and did not recognize the serious financial problems that would arise from finding and financing ships, and from dealing with the maritime unions — which, I was to learn, were utterly indifferent to the survival of the company that provided their employment.

The search for a third ship had begun back in 1962 when I realized that if we were to continue to grow, we needed more cruise space to support our cruise-tour programs. It seemed logical that we build a ship from the keel up, designed especially for our Inside Passage needs. Phil Spaulding, a friend and neighbor with a fine reputation as a marine architect, had designed ships for the Alaska State Ferry System and the Black Ball Line. I asked him to draw plans for a cruise ship to be called the *"Alaska Queen"*: about 350 feet long, accommodating 250 passengers. The projected cost was in the neighborhood of $3.5 million — in those days, that was a pretty nice neighborhood.

We took Spaulding's design to Victoria Machinery Depot (VMD) and negotiated a contract for $3.7 million to deliver the ship fully equippped and ready to sail. With this agreement understood, I went back to my old partners at the White Pass & Yukon Route railroad and asked them to come in once again as my guarantor, this time for a million dollars; I would finance the balance. They agreed, so we went ahead with plans to build the ship. VMD set up a construction schedule and ordered the steel.

All seemed to be going smoothly until one day I received a telephone call from Harold Hudson, president of VMD. He told me his engineers had gone over Spaulding's drawings for the *Alaska Queen*. He said her design was so top heavy that she would be unstable; the only solution would be to build the superstructure of aluminum, not steel. When I asked how much this change would cost, he said, "Don't worry about it. I'll help you finance it because I don't want to lose the job."

I asked him again what the difference would be. When he answered, "A million dollars, more or less," I went into shock. With or without his help in financing the extra cost, I would eventually need another million dollars I had not anticipated. My projections didn't indicate that I would generate that much extra income. I telephoned Frank Brown, president of the White Pass & Yukon. When I explained the situation, all he said was, "Thanks for telling us."

Then I went back to Victoria where Harold Hudson took me to lunch at his club and assured me that he would stand behind the additional cost — at least to the extent that he would do all he could to assure that his bank would extend me the additional credit. We went to see his banker and when we got to the bottom line, they wanted me to sign a note for $4.8 million dollars. That was too much. I had jumped through a lot of hoops but when it came to numbers that big, I balked. What would happen if — after they started building the ship — they discovered another unanticipated half million or so? I would be in so far over my head that I would not be able to make the payments, and someone else would own my company. I told Hudson I could not afford to risk that possibility. My entire future was tied up in this shipbuilding venture; the risk was too great. I backed out of the deal.

When Hudson protested that the steel had already been purchased and delivered to the yard, I told him I was sorry about that. Hudson still had his steel; I had already paid the architect $25,000 and had nothing to show for it. Those are the risks one takes in business. The contract cancellation made headlines in Victoria newspapers: ALASKA CRUISE LINE CANCELS ORDER FOR SHIP. I was saddened by the whole episode and was sorry that it happened when it did, during the depression of 1962. But it couldn't be helped.

After the meeting with Hudson and his bankers, I flew to Vancouver where Ray Kusler, vice president of administration for Alaska Cruise Lines, and I met at offices of the White Pass & Yukon Route to see Frank Brown and Bert Freisen. None of the participants will forget that meeting, ever. The discussion began with afternoon tea, served elegantly according to British-Canadian custom — sterling silver, fine china, the works. Sipping my tea, I explained to Brown and Freisen why I would not build the ship. Then to my utter disbelief Brown told me that his company had not been convinced that they wanted to go along with my proposal and would not have supported me if I had gone ahead with the $4.8 million commitment. My dismay at his announcement was so sudden and so overwhelming that when I lowered my teacup to the saucer I broke it. Then when I asked him about his agreement to put up a million dollar guarantee, he said, "Well, you see, Mr. West, you didn't have our signatures on any kind of document; if you had committed your company to another million, we would have backed out."

It now occurred to me that had I gone ahead and signed the $4.8 million contract offered in Victoria *and* had the White Pass & Yukon Route then withdrawn its support, Alaska Cruise Lines would have been ripe for a quick take over. I had telephoned Brown from Victoria and explained the situation. He had said nothing then to discourage me from assuming the additional indebtedness. The White Pass & Yukon Route owned the railroad between Skagway and Whitehorse. They also controlled almost all other surface transportation within the Yukon Territory. My cruise ships and tour operation in Alaska would have made a handsome addition to their near-monopoly.

With my recognition of the situation that I had avoided, I erupted — loudly, unmistakably, and I believe eloquently — as I questioned the morality and ancestry of my stunned former partners. This unscheduled part of the meeting culminated with my overturning the sterling silver tea service on Brown's desk and exiting his office, a stunned Ray Kusler in tow.

The rift with the White Pass & Yukon was wide and irreparable. We had used that company's services to carry our tour customers through the Yukon Territory, but when the tourist season opened the following spring, we were prepared to bypass the WP&Y. As mentioned in an earlier chapter, the White Pass from Skagway is not the only route through the mountains from the northern end of the Inside Passage to the interior. Another pass, the Chilkat, leads from Haines, a short distance from Skagway, to Haines

Junction, 155 miles north on the Alaska Highway. We had already used this highway in a "Golden Horseshoe" tour pattern — Skagway, Whitehorse, Haines — that had proved very popular.

Although our Alaska Hyway Tours division did not have authority to transport passengers to or from the Yukon Territory, there was no restriction on our carrying travelers *through* the Yukon. And that's what we did: we took them from Haines, Alaska, through the Yukon to Fairbanks, Alaska, with an overnight stop at Alas/kon Border Lodge. The result of this was that BYN, the White Pass & Yukon bus subsidiary, disappeared from the highway within a couple of years; without our business feeding their routes they were not able to sustain their service. When BYN eventually lapsed, our buses began to operate into Whitehorse as well as Haines. We offered both routes as options for our tour passengers.

Chilkat Pass was an ancient Indian trail used by the coastal Chilkat tribe to trade with the Athabascans in the interior. Several years *before* the gold rush, an enterprising adventurer named Jack Dalton had explored the Chilkat trail. Then after the gold rush started, he negotiated an agreement with the Indians which allowed him to improve and extend the trail. He then gave it his name — the Dalton Trail — and established a "toll road" to the Klondike gold fields. In 1898 and 1899, before completion of the White Pass & Yukon Route railway, his trail was the better way to deliver much-needed meat-on-the-hoof to the Klondike. The trail led from Pyramid Harbor near Haines Mission to Five Finger Rapids on the Yukon River. Though longer than the White Pass from Skagway, Dalton's route was well maintained, easier to travel, and could be used safely from early spring until late fall.

Thousands traveled his toll road during those early years. Dalton charged by "the head" and carried a shotgun to enforce his collections: $2.00 each for cattle, $2.50 for horses, $150 for a person. After the Gold Rush he switched to other business ventures, including diamond mining in British Guiana — and finally reached the end of his trail in San Francisco, age 89.

In 1904, the U.S. government established a military post at Port Chilkoot, one-half mile west of Haines. Later, during World War II, Dalton's trail was improved and became an automobile road, an alternative to the White Pass & Yukon railroad. That's just what I needed: an alternative to the White Pass & Yukon. We started taking our travelers through Haines-Port Chilkoot instead of Skagway. The picturesque army post looked (and still looks today) much as it did when first built. Its former officers' quarters had been converted by Clarence and Hilma Mattson into a comfortable "frontier" hotel, the Halsingland — owned and operated today by Arne Olsson, Hilda's nephew, and Arne's wife Joyce.

The Chilkat Indians, under the direction of Carl Heinmiller, conduct an Indian arts and crafts program that is interesting to visitors, as are the

Chilkats' performances of Indian songs and dances. Haines was, and is, an attractive alternative to Skagway. Moreover, Chilkat Pass, which the Haines Highway traverses, is one of the most spectacular motor routes in the North Country, with stark, snow- and glacier-capped peaks jutting up in all directions.

In 1963 I had asked Ralph Johansen, Pan American World Airways district sales manager in Seattle, to join Westours. I felt that his extensive sales experience would be needed to help market our expanded needs after we acquired an additional ship. When the third ship did not materialize, Johansen decided to leave Westours (in 1965) and went on to establish his own tour company, Johansen Royal Tours, which concentrated primarily on motorcoach tours to the Canadian Rockies and which developed a fine reputation among travel agents across the country. When he retired, Johansen sold his company to Princess Tours.

It was during those years that the greatest natural disaster in Alaska's recorded history struck the state's Gulf Coast region — the "Good Friday Earthquake" of 1964. The quake destroyed much of downtown Anchorage and wiped out Valdez entirely. Old Valdez was abandoned and a new community built several miles away. The quake, which spread shock waves over 700,000 square miles, also triggered the highest seismic sea wave ever recorded. An undersea slide near Shoup Glacier in Port Valdez created a wave that toppled trees 100 feet above the sea and deposited silt and sand 225 feet above sea level. The Sea of Japan developed 12-foot waves as a result of the earthquake.

Our entire family was in Hawaii when the earthquake hit Alaska. The Hawaiians expected a *tsunami* — a great tidal wave — to strike the islands. We were warned to stay off the streets and were safe enough in the penthouse apartment of a tall building in Honolulu, but we were terribly worried about our two youngest children, Ral and Richard, who had gone to a movie. We couldn't leave the building to search for them — police and the military were shooing people off the streets.

After an agonizing wait, the phone rang; it was a Japanese man who had gone to the theater to pick up his own children. He had realized that our children were strangers to the area and would not know what to do, so he took them to his home — on high ground — until the *tsunami* alert was over. Richard was then eleven and Ral nine. I will always remember the thoughtfulness and kindness of that man.

When I learned of the earthquake damage in Alaska, I left Hawaii and flew directly to Anchorage. The Westward Hotel lobby was a shambles, but the hotel still had rooms available. Everett Patton had driven down from

Fairbanks to meet me. Together, we drove to Valdez to inspect the Valdez Hotel where we held reservations for the tourist season.

A control center had been established at Copper Center, on the Richardson Highway north of Valdez. Security for the area was directed by an old friend George Ashby, owner of Copper Center Lodge. Patton and I were waved through the roadblocks and allowed to enter shattered Valdez. The lobby of the Hotel Valdez was under water but hotel owner, Bill Wyatt, was able to give us a second-floor room. I assured him of our support and encouragement in rebuilding and had every confidence that he would provide some kind of accommodations for our travelers that coming season. Wyatt was able to get financing to build another hotel in *new* Valdez. He first called it the New Valdez Hotel but later changed the name to The Wyatt House, and eventually sold to Sheffield Hotels. The hotel is now named Sheffield Valdez.

I never realized how important friendships could be until I went to Alaska after that earthquake. I knew the people, they knew me. We were concerned about one another's welfare and we worked together as a team. Everyone helped. It was a heart-warming revelation.

We still needed one more cruise ship. I instituted a world-wide search for a vessel and late in 1965 contacted the Greek cruise company Sun Line, which had purchased the sister ship of the *Glacier Queen* and *Yukon Star* and transformed that third corvette into a truly luxurious assenger ship (as only the Greeks can). I fell in love with the trim ship the moment I set eyes on her. The Greeks had christened her the *Stella Maris* — the first ship of that name.

We purchased the *Stella Maris* in January, 1964, renamed her the *Westar* (pronounced "Wee-star"), arranged insurance through Lloyds of London, and sent our crew to Piraeus, port of Athens, to bring the new Alaska Cruise Line vessel to Vancouver. On her way through the Mediterranean, the ship stopped at the island of Sardinia for fuel. It was there that disaster struck. A refueling explosion set the *Westar* afire; she was totally destroyed and two of the ship's engineers perished.

The deaths and the terrible fire need not have happened had crewmen in charge of refueling behaved responsibly. The fuel line from the shoreside tank to the vessel was designed to be secured to the ship's fuel port by five bolts; only three were made fast. When the line filled with fuel, pumped at high pressure, it began to shake and pulsate. This whipping motion finally snapped the three bolts, and thousands of gallons of pressurized fuel sprayed over the ship before the pumps could be shut down. Fuel entered engine room ventilators that had been left open because of hot weather. When the spray of oil blasted into the engine room, the vessel — a floating bomb — flared almost instantly into a great ugly torch.

Quickly cutting the lines, the Italian dockside crew allowed the burning ship to drift out with the tide, saving the pier from damage and also assuring that fire-fighting apparatus could not reach the burning *Westar*. She was a goner, drifting in flames, sending great billows of greasy black smoke into the sky. She beached herself and burned to the water line, a sad and needless loss.

I was in Manila when I learned of the catastrophe. I had gone to the Philippines on a trade mission for the Seattle Chamber of Commerce, accompanied by Jim Binkley, the Fairbanks riverboat captain. When Jack Musiel telephoned me the terrible news, I abandoned the trade mission to fly home. Ray Kusler, who was in Piraeus at the time of the accident, flew to Sardinia to see what could be done. The ship was beyond help and he returned to Seattle in near shock — bringing only the ship's bell as a memento of the accident.

With the loss of the *Westar*, I had abandoned immediate plans to add a third vessel to the Alaska Cruise Lines fleet but retained an English ships' broker, Mike Hickling, to conduct a more leisurely search for the right vessel. He located several candidates, and I or senior members of Westours' staff traveled frequently to Norway, Sweden, Denmark and other parts of Europe to inspect likely ships that he uncovered — an expensive and time-consuming endeavor.

Eventually we located what we were looking for, the Hamburg-built *Woppen-von Hamburg*. Designed to exacting German engineering standards, the shallow-draft vessel, originally built to cruise the Rhine River and carry passengers to the Channel Islands, was now owned by Nomikos Line of Greece, who renamed her the *Delos* and used her in the Mediterranean and Aegean seas.

In August of 1967 Marguerite and I made a Greek Island cruise on the *Delos*; and once again I fell in love with a ship. Powered by an efficient diesel-electric system, she was about three hundred feet long and accommodated one hundred sixty-five passengers. Spit-and-polish clean and in every sense a luxury vessel, the ship sported beautiful woodwork, lovely public rooms, large and comfortable cabins, air conditioning, and spacious deck areas. She even had a small swimming pool on the after deck. The *Delos* was ideal for our needs, so we bought her.

Renamed the *Polar Star*, the new vessel went into service as Alaska Cruise Lines' flagship in 1968, Captain Shepherd in command. Canadian maritime law required extensive changes in the crew's compartments and steel bulkheads and general fireproofing throughout the vessel. The more than one million dollars in improvements brought the total cost of the *Polar Star* to $3.5 million. She proved an efficient, happy ship. Crew and passengers loved her.

Once again, it seemed, our course was full steam ahead.

We Need A Fourth Ship

For two years, the three ships of Alaska Cruise Lines provided enough passenger space to keep pace with our cruise-tour sales. But as business continued to increase, we were in the happy position of bringing in more customers than we could handle. By 1969 I realized that yet another ship was needed. The search was on and our English ships' broker, Mike Hickling, discovered a Spanish vessel, the *Cabo Izarra*, under contract to Thomas Cook. The *Cabo* sailed summers in the Mediterranean, winters in the Caribbean.

Her price was $5 million. My financial advisors recommended "going public" with a stock issue by the umbrella corporation Westours. We purchased the ship under yet another corporate entity, Westline, Inc., created largely so that the *Cabo Izarra* could operate in other parts of the world besides Alaska: we thought she represented too large an investment to sit idle during the winter season, and we planned to sail her in the Inside Passage summers and in the South Pacific winters. The ship, whose previous home port had been Barcelona, came complete with a Spanish crew. I had signed a contract with her former owners to keep that Spanish crew for another year. Having a foreign crew required that we register the ship as a foreign-flag vessel; so the *Cabo*, renamed the *West Star*, was registered in Liberia. I was advised that the foreign registry gave me legal rights to operate with a foreign crew in North American waters, as long as sailings were not between two U.S. ports.

That's not how it worked out. The paragraph immediately above contains *all* of the ingredients that ultimately fused and forced my loss of Westours.

No sooner had I signed the order for the ship and committed the full financial resources of Westours — I had "bet the company" one more time — than the Seamans International Union of North America came down on us. The union bluntly informed me that it would not allow the ship to operate in Alaskan waters unless she carried an SIU crew. It was like being clubbed from behind; I had no inkling that I was going to be hit. We had no intention to change the crew structure of the other three ships. But the *West Star* was a deep-draft hull; only by sailing her twelve months of the year could we hope to amortize our $5 million investment. This required using her in foreign waters with a foreign crew.

In that same year, 1969, contract negotiations were under way with the SIU for a new agreement covering crews of the other three ships — the *Polar Star, Yukon Star* and *Glacier Queen.* These ships were Canadian flag. The stumbling block to interminable negotiations with the union was always the Spanish ship. Our contract with the previous owners required that we retain the original crew for at least one year. We were legally prohibited from complying with union demands that we man her with an SIU crew. The crux of the union's position was that we use SIU crews on all four ships, or they would permit none of our ships to sail in North American waters. The power to govern is not limited to the government. The union was a governing force that operated outside the law.

We had previously informed the union that we were buying a fourth ship and that it would be under foreign registry with a foreign crew. We had explained that we would use the ship in the South Pacific and Mexico as well as in Alaska. We did not try to hide anything. The SIU had made no objections when we told them of our plans; they waited until we put our money down and all the company assets were at risk. Then when we were extended as far as we could go, the union as much as told us they would put us out of business if we tried to sail with a foreign crew.

In the meantime, the travel season drew near. We were selling cruise and tour reservations at a great rate, booking hundreds of passengers on or ships. And while the *West Star* crossed the Atlantic and made her way through the Panama Canal into North American waters, the union had effectively impounded the *Glacier Queen* and *Yukon Star*, which were surrounded by pickets and out of the water in a Vancouver dry dock. Nor did the union intend to yield us the *Polar Star*, tied to a dock in Victoria.

Looking back, I can see clearly now why I made the decisions that I did and why those decisions, based on my trust in the SIU, were wrong. I simply could not comprehend the unreasoning stance of the SIU leaders. Their uncompromising position flew in the face of all common sense. They were prepared — eager, it seemed — to throw scores of their own members out of work, as though they wanted those men to lose their jobs in order to dramatize the union leaders' position. In 1984 fourteen large cruise ships carried 150,000 passengers to Alaska — all were foreign registry, manned by foreign crews, employing not a single SIU member. Those members, at the direction of their leaders, picketed their only employer out of existence.

What to do? Passengers were booked; we needed ships. Through a friend, Raymond Piscatella, president of a New York-based tour company, The Leisure Corporation, I managed to sub-charter the Greek ship *Orpheus*. We agreed — in a joint venture with Leisure — to use the *Orpheus* in Alaska that summer and to Mexico the following winter. We agreed on a joint promotional budget of $600,000 to be divided equally. The people at Leisure insisted that they were the promotional experts and that they should place the ads and prepare sales literature; we were so busy with other concerns that we told them to go ahead. At their request I sent them a certified check for $300,000, which they received on a Friday.

On Monday they declared bankruptcy.

Leisure International Tours, headed by a former executive vice president of ASTA, went out of business with $300,000 of our money — and no program to Mexico. We were left with the full burden to promote Mexico and to fulfill the charter of the *Orpheus*.

We had negotiated for the *Orpheus* in March of 1970. The ship sailed April 1 from Portugal, nine thousand miles from Seattle where, in mid-May, passengers were scheduled to embark for Alaska. Anxiously, we followed her progress down the coast of Africa to the Canary Islands, across the Atlantic to the Caribbean, through the Panama Canal, up the west coast of Mexico, and then up the west coast of the United States to Puget Sound. She arrived in Seattle's Elliott Bay at 6:00 a.m. of the day she was supposed to sail for Alaska with a full load of passengers. Union trucks would not approach her; we provisioned the ship ourselves. My family and Westours' office employees drove U-drive trucks and loaded her. I remember watching some of the office staff, white with flour dust, as they shouldered sacks of flour up the gangway. Passengers embarked at both Seattle and Victoria and that night were cruising through the Strait of Georgia off Vancouver Island, Alaska bound.

Meanwhile, unidentified men threatened wives and children of our ships' officers and company officials. We were followed, afoot and in automobiles, wherever we went. I, myself, was jostled and roughed up in the street, apparently in what were attempts to provoke physical violence. Once while standing on the dock, I was approached by a huge, burly man who bumped me with a body block, knocking me about six feet toward the edge of the dock. He said, "Can you swim, Mr. West?" I said, "I can swim, but if I do you're going with me." I began to carry a weapon and was quite prepared to use it. All the while attorneys attempted to settle the union disagreement, resorting to injunctions in an unsuccessful attempt to halt picketing and threats of violence at dockside.

With the *Orpheus* and *West Star* in service, we could manage without the two smaller ships, the *Yukon Star* and *Glacier Queen*. But we needed the *Polar Star*, incarcerated by the maritime union at the dock in Victoria. We needed her badly. To get her would require "a little innovation." In a secret meeting attended by myself, Jack Musiel, Ray Kusler, and our marine superintendent, Harry Case, we decided the most innovative action we could take would be to "steal" her. And that's what we did. I hired a non-union tug and a non-union crew to sail up Puget Sound to Victoria. At midnight on a Saturday night the blacked-out tug and its small band of men nudged alongside the *Polar Star* in Victoria Harbor. A crew slipped aboard to secure a towing hawser and cut the ship's dockside lines. Within minutes, she was under tow, gliding out of Victoria Harbor and across the Strait of Juan de Fuca to Puget Sound and Seattle. I've always wished that I could have been there to view the expressions on those pickets' faces when that dark, silent ship slipped away from the dock and out of Victoria harbor. To carry through this bit of innovation we had no alternative but to forego certain formalities — that ship never went through Customs.

The *Polar Star* required underwater stern-end work. This was done between Saturday night and Monday morning at Lockheed Shipyards in Seattle. Before dawn on Monday we moved her out of the shipyard to a safe moorage in Tacoma, a few miles south of Seattle, where other necessary work was completed. Wherever the ship went, the pickets followed.

If the Canadian-flag *Polar Star* was to operate, her registry had to be changed. Spending large sums of money, hiring attorneys, and wading through bureaucratic swamps, we managed to change the ship's registry to Panamanian and to secure the proper flag certificate. This done, we chartered a plane to bring a Spanish crew from Barcelona to Seattle.

So, as it turned out, during that summer of 1970 we sailed three ships to Alaska: a Greek ship with a Greek crew, a Panamanian ship with a Spanish crew, and a Liberian ship with a Spanish crew. Because union trucks would not cross picket lines, Westours' office personnel and my family continued to stock the ships with provisions. As a last resort, I called for police protection when pickets tried to prevent passengers from boarding. Non-union men cast off lines at Washington ports and then flew with me in my private airplane to Victoria to take the lines when our ships arrived there. At other times — when the union would not permit ships to dock — our vessels anchored in the harbors and we ferried passengers ashore by lighter or tender.

Although we beat the strike, in the long run it was a Pyrrhic victory — wasteful, senseless and ugly. I hope this story will demonstrate, for all to know, how ruthless, power-hungry, and senseless union leaders brazenly scuttled the Canadian and U.S. maritime industry. We read and hear — today — of the dwindling influence of the union movement. A large portion of the responsibility for this goes to the union members who chose the wrong leaders — if it is true that they had a voice in the choosing.

Adversity is not without its lighter moments, and some of the stop-gap measures we used during the union ugliness were more comic than tragic. For a time, as we attempted to teach the Spanish galley crew the ways of North American cooking, the comedy resembled a Marx Brothers movie.

Marguerite recruited a Spanish-speaking woman from our tour department to translate menus so that galley people would know what to prepare for each meal; even the chief cook did not speak English. The same Spanish-speaking lady sailed with the ship and schooled the galley crew in what they would be serving. Even so, for a while there we thought we had Groucho, Harpo and Chico running back and forth between the dining room and the galley. Marguerite will never forget seeing the first breakfast plate being carried through the galley door. The order had been for hash-browned potatoes, eggs over easy, and sausages. In Spanish this translated to boiled potatoes, an egg still in its shell, and hot dogs. Frozen pies that should have been thawed and baked were served *un*baked. The galley crew, unable to read the ''open'' labels on paper milk cartons, simply whacked the tops off with a knife.

On the other hand, when the cooks prepared dishes they knew — paella and other traditional Spanish dishes — they did very well, indeed. In fact, we eventually simply changed the menus so that they could prepare the foods they were accustomed to.

That first sailing of the *Polar Star* was more hectic than any other in my memory. The storeroom flooded (someone left a valve open). Deck chairs bought from Sears to replace those guarded by picket lines in Vancouver were so light and fragile that half of them blew off the deck and into the sea. There was no end to the problems.

We had decided to send the *Polar Star* on twelve-day voyages across the Gulf of Alaska to Seward, duplicating the sailings of the old Alaska Steam ships many years earlier. All went well as long as the *Polar Star* cruised through protected Inside Passage waters. Then the ship left Icy Strait, rounded Cape Spencer, and encountered gigantic seas in the Gulf of Alaska. The small, shallow-draft vessel, perfect for the Inside Passage, was not designed for storms in the open ocean, and she behaved accordingly. The captain, in his wisdom, simply reversed his course to Icy Strait, planning to wait out the bad weather. After a twenty-four hour delay, Gulf of Alaska seas were still too heavy. He cancelled the cruise and returned to Puget Sound.

The only honorable thing I could do — the voyage having been a catastrophe — was to refund the price of the cruise to every passenger on board, a costly decision, but at that point I was losing so much money that a little more didn't seem to make much difference. I stood, myself, in the salon of the *Polar Star* and handed refund checks to the passengers. Even after I had refunded what people had paid me for the cruise, there were some who asked that I also pay for their airline tickets from Seattle back to their home cities. This I could not do.

And that was only the beginning. I now owned or held under charter three cruise ships that must operate year around if the company was to survive. We had decided that during winter months we would cruise the *Orpheus* in Mexico and the *West Star* in the South pacific. And since those two ships carried more than five hundred passengers between them, they provided all the space we would need to support our summer Alaska tours. So we decided to take the *Polar Star* out of Alaska entirely and use her year around in a cruise from Tahiti through the Society Islands. We called this cruise "Tahiti SeaVenture," and at the conclusion of the 1970 Alaska summer season sent the *Polar Star*, renamed the *Pacific Star*, to Papeete. The little ship, which had been perfect for the calm waters of Alaska's Inside Passage, was equally well suited to the lagoons of Tahiti, Moorea, Bora Bora, Huahine, Raiatea, and Rangiroa.

The *West Star* South Pacific cruise, which also began in December of 1970, seemed like an equally marvelous idea. It *was* a marvelous idea. The ship sailed back and forth between Tahiti and Fiji, calling enroute at Rarotonga in the Cook Islands, American and Western Samoa, Vava'u and Tonga — eleven days in Paradise. Life aboard ship was informal, reflecting the casual atmosphere of the South Seas. The cruise connected with airline schedules at Tahiti and Fiji, allowing travelers to insert the one-way, eleven-day voyage into an ongoing tour to other parts of the South Pacific.

Our winter Mexico cruises aboard the **Orpheus** were scheduled to sail from San Diego to Mazatlan, Puerto Vallarta, Cabo San Lucas and other ports along the Mexican Riviera. It was a good itinerary and the *Orpheus* was a good ship; she still sails today in the Mediterranean.

Our plans seemed so reasonable at the time. The South Pacific cruises promised to be two of the most attractive travel ideas ever offered. The Mexican Riviera has since become one of the world's most popular cruise destinations. So often — before — I had surmounted trouble and *made* things work. But the troubles that lay ahead were on a grander scale, involving grander sums of money. The year 1970 was a down year for the economy. We were in new and unfamiliar parts of the world and had much to learn about sailing in foreign waters. Start-up costs were far higher than anticipated.

The decision to buy the Spanish-crewed *Cabo Izarra* had pitched me headlong into a succession of crises that my habits of winning had not prepared me for.

Starting school: Chuck, age 5, with sister Mary Lou, age 7.

Chuck, age 15.

U.S. Air Force Pilot Training School, St. George, Utah, July 1942. From left: Chuck West, Larry Frye, Bob Brewer, George Banton.

Western Airlines district and regional sales managers, Spring, 1941. Standing, from left: Roy Thompson, George Keyser, Charles James, Art Kelly. Kneeling: Tom Tobin, Richard Dick, Chuck West, Guy Talbot, Tom Murphy.

In Western Airlines uniform, during "Operation Sourdough," 1942.
With Norm Geiger, right, in Kunming, 1944.
C.N.A.C. pilots, Kunming, China, 1944. From left: Bob Miller, Chuck West, Bob Heilig.
Returning home from China-Burma-India Theater, February 1945.

Chuck and Marguerite's wedding, Claremont, California, 1943: On left is Marguerite's mother, Carrie Lee. On right are Chuck's parents, Mae and Louis LeFlore West.

Parents 50th wedding anniversary, 1961. On right is Chuck's sister, Mary Lou Laws.

Marguerite holding Charles, with Barbara, left, and CarraLee, Fairbanks, 1947.

West children at Magnolia home in Seattle, Easter 1959. Behind, from left, Barbara, Charles, and CarraLee; front, Richard and Ral.

With Marguerite and CarraLee before leaving for China in 1944.

Chuck and Marguerite at Fairbanks Inn opening, May, 1964.

Chuck with sons Charles, center, and Dick at Wien Arctic Hotel in Kotzebue, Summer 1960.

Bush pilot West picks up a passenger.

Loading a dog team aboard a Boeing 247D. Chuck West is in doorway of plane. Dog mushers were Jeff Studdert and his wife.

With Norm Geiger, right, in front of Second Avenue office, Fairbanks, 1948.

Norm Geiger, left, with Chuck and new Chrysler sightseeing limo, which Geiger drove up the Alaska Highway. The Wests' log cabin Fairbanks home is behind trees. Parked behind Chrysler is the DeSoto Suburban, Arctic Alaska Tours' first sightseeing vehicle.

Chuck West with Celia Hunter in front of Arctic Alaska Travel Service First Avenue office, Fairbanks. Spring, 1947.

Chuck West, left, and Wien pilot Bill English, transfer a patient from Bellanca to ambulance at Weeks Field, Fairbanks.

Alaska Visitors Association board of directors, 1951. Standing, from left: Everett Patton, Alaska Sightseeing Company; Ray Peterson, Peterson Airways; Chuck West; Frank Downey, White Pass & Yukon Route; Henry Green, Alaska Steamship Company; Cot Hayes, Northwest Airlines. Seated, Helen Monsen, publisher, Juneau Empire; Bernice Stokke, Mitkoff Hotel, Petersburg; Jack Whaley, Wien Alaska Airlines; O. F. Benecke, Alaska Coastal Airlines; Bernice Morgan, m/v *Northwind,* Juneau.

Taking delivery in Seattle of three Flexible buses for Alaska Hyway Tours, 1956. From left; Everett Patton, Brad Phillips Jim Binkley.

The *Yukon Star* approaching Haines dock, 1962.

Chuck West with Alaska Cruise Lines captains, from left, Ernest Shepherd, *Polar Star*; William McCombe Jr., *Glacier Queen*; and William McCombe Sr., *Yukon Star*. 1958-59 period.

Presiding over the International Conference of ASTA in Tokyo, 1969.

Polar Star in Tracy Arm Fjord.

WESTOURS MANAGEMENT TEAM 1970: (Left to right.) Front row: Howard C. Hansen, *Vice President Agency and Interline Sales;* H. J. Musiel, *Senior Vice President;* C. B. West, *President;* H. F. Case, *General Manager, Marine Division;* John Hickman, *General Manager, Hotel Division;* Bob Davis, *Director, Advertising and Public Relations;* F. Ashida, *Director Sales Planning and Operations;* M. W. Freeman, *General Manager, Motor Coach Division;* R. C. Davies, *Director, Pacific Cruise-Tour Operations;* A. T. Wendells (standing, center), *Vice President for Administration, Secretary-General Counsel;* G. G. Hickock, *Manager, Industrial Relations;* A. K. Lanterman, *Financial Vice President, Treasurer.*

With Jack Musiel, right, at Westours in 1968. Making plans for expansion.
Receiving the Golden Plate Award.
The M.V. *West Star*.

Chuck with future Alaska Sightseeing/Cruise West President, Richard G. (Dick) West, age 13, before flying to Alaska in 1966.

Chuck, age 78, flying his glider near Borrego Springs.

Chuck and Dick West today.

Sheltered Seas in Tracy Arm.

Spirit of Glacier Bay near Reid Glacier.

Glacier Seas near Cox Glacier in Barry Arm
of Prince William Sound.

Spirit of '98 in Tracy Arm.
Spirit of Discovery in LeConte Glacier Fjord.
Spirit of Alaska at entrance to Princess Louisa Inlet.

At the West cabin, Paradise Cove, Haines, 1984.

PART III:

ZENITH AND DECLINE —
I LOSE WESTOURS TO SAVE IT

Mission To Rotterdam —
Encounter And Loss

In 1967 I was elected to a two-year term as vice president of the American Society of Travel Agents (ASTA). Subsequently, in 1969, I was elected to a two-year term as president of ASTA. For four years my attention was divided between ASTA and Westours. During this period I came to rely on others to explore decisions that I did not have time to explore myself. Too often I was busy preparing yet another speech to be delivered at yet another conference in yet another part of the world — during a period that proved disastrous to the future of my own company.

In 1969 and 1970 I presided over international ASTA conferences in Tokyo and Amsterdam. These conferences were attended by thousands of travel agents and by top executives who represent the world's most prestigious airlines, cruise companies, tour operators, hotel chains, government tourist offices — the entire travel industry.

And I was the big cheese at the crest of my career. I rode in limousines, occupied suites in the finest hotels, spent all kinds of money. I was feted at banquets and invited to speak at meetings and conferences wherever I went. Honorary certificates, awards, plaques and scrolls adorned the walls of my office in Seattle. Some were humorous; some were records of solid achievement. I was presented the Golden Plate Award in 1970 as Travel Man of the Year. (Others who received Golden Plate awards that year included Terry Bradshaw, Tommy Orr, and Shirley Temple Black.) From the Australian National Tourist Office I received a replica of Captain Cook's sword: Cook had crossed great distances and explored the world; I had helped latter-day travelers do the same. I had created a large and successful travel corporation and was president of the world's largest and most prestigious society of travel agents.

And I was beginning to believe my own publicity.

Decisions impacting the future of Westours during that period were wrong. Whether I would have gone through with some of those decisions had my energy and time not been diverted by ASTA — who can say? Whatever the case, Westours was in trouble when the ASTA conference convened in Amsterdam in the fall of 1970. And I was too busy to realize just how deep that trouble was.

At one of the many social events attendant to the Amsterdam conference, I met Nico Van der Vorm of Holland-America Line. In the course of small talk Van der Vorm asked if he might call on me to talk "a little business." Knowing of his affiliation with Holland-America, I agreed even though conference sessions and other meetings imposed a killing schedule. Van der Vorm later called for an appointment and entered my suite just as another group of visitors were leaving. I was late for another meeting but we talked for several minutes.

He wanted to know if I was interested in selling Westours or merging with Holland-America Cruises. He said that Holland-America was interested in the North American market, that Westours was a highly successful operation with passenger ships, hotels, a motorcoach company, a good name, and useful connections with the airlines and surface transportation companies. He said that he was also impressed by my work as president of ASTA. When I asked how he saw Westours and Holland-America complementing each other's operations, he said that Westours excelled in marketing, while Holland-America was experienced in cruises. He thought we would make a good team, particularly in the Pacific Northwest.

As we left the room my words were, "Well, let's explore it further when we have more time."

He said that if the opportunity for further discussion did not present itself in Amsterdam, he would be happy to come to New York or Seattle. We shook hands and went our separate ways. During the waning days of the conference we encountered each other at several social affairs, but had no time to talk seriously in the midst of the tightly scheduled ASTA conference.

Bear in mind that I was still flying high on the prestige of the ASTA presidency, convinced that I had at last "made it" — that my company and I were powers to be dealt with in North American tourism. At the Amsterdam conference I was the central figure in an industry I had served for many years, my mood so elevated that I felt invulnerable. Had I only known how vulnerable I was! I had spent so much time preparing for the conference that I was out of touch with the condition of my own company, aware of hints and undercurrents but oblivious to the immediacy of disaster.

To illustrate the level of my mood — after the conference had concluded,

I escorted Marguerite to the showrooms of Jaguar dealers in London and, on the spot, bought her a twelve-cylinder, 2X2 XKE sports car, saying offhandedly, "Oh, hell — it's only $12,000 (a lot more then than now), and you've wanted one for years. Now you have it!" I wrote out a check for the full amount and ordered the car delivered in Seattle. Had I known the true state of affairs at Westours, I would not so much as have bought a set of tires for that car.

The first day in the office following the ASTA convention was one of unmitigated gloom. Kirk Lanterman, our controller, spelled out the company's position: revenues were down, expenses were up — way up. Lanterman had joined us the preceding summer after Ray Kusler left, unhappy with the way things were going. Kusler's departure was a blow to the stability of the company, particularly at a time when expert financial counsel was urgently needed. Lanterman, who came to us from Price-Waterhouse, had been instructed to trim expenses to the bone; and he had done just that, but the company was fast running out of money.

The month was November. On February 1, just one fiscal quarter away, Westours owed a million-dollar payment on the *West Star*. While the net worth of the company was sound, there were serious obligations that had to be met, and Westours had run out of security for loans. The *Yukon Star* and *Glacier Queen* were out of service, blockaded by the union. The *Pacific Star* was an asset but other properties were not fully paid for. Hotels were mortgaged. We owed money on buses. There were payrolls to meet.

All that was left were my personal assets: securities, stocks and bonds, our home, life insurance, savings, and my ownership in Westours. I had put them all on the line before. Now I put them on the line again. The bank loaned me $900,000 on our family's personal assets. I told Marguerite: "It will be like starting over again. It's time to show faith in what we have been trying to build all these years."

The infusion of cash provided operating capital but did nothing to offset the whopping million-dollar ship payment due in February. I needed more cash and thought first of the tentative nibble made by Van der Vorm in Amsterdam. In response to my call he said that he planned a trip to New York in December. I wanted to see him sooner than that and urged him to reschedule his trip. I told him I was interested in selling or merging my company and would like to see him before Christmas. He said he would call me back — I spent several anxious days waiting for that call. When he finally telephoned, he told me he would be in New York within a week, registered at the Hilton Hotel.

In the meantime I had learned that Nico Van der Vorm was chairman of the board for Holland-America and that he and his family owned substantial blocks of Holland-America stock. If *anyone* in that enormous organization could make the decision that would bail out the ailing Westours,

Nico Van der Vorm was the man. At our New York meeting, I explained our situation. I told him the financial crisis had caught me off guard, that Westours was a viable company with a good business record and a worth of about fifteen million dollars. I suggested that Westours sell perhaps $2 million in shares to Holland-America and that a marriage of Westours' marketing experience with Holland-America's cruise ships would benefit both companies and keep Westours a vital corporation.

Van der Vorm's face revealed nothing. When he spoke it was with reservation. He said he would have to talk with his financial people and would get back to me. I suggested that he send his financial advisors to Seattle to see me. He responded: "Perhaps we can work something out, possibly sometime after the first of the year." I wanted to scream at the man, "For God's sake, I need help NOW, not after the first of the year." But all I said was that in the meantime I would have to look elsewhere for the help I needed.

That was not a bluff. Paquet Cruises had expressed interest in my company. I flew to Paris to talk with Paquet's company officers. And though the French company was genuinely interested in investing in Westours, they would not be hurried. Time was short. I contacted a British-owned company based in Hong Kong and arranged a meeting in Seattle with their representatives — who turned out to be even slower moving than Paquet.

At this point, just before the holiday season of 1970, I said, "To hell with it," and took the family on a cruise to Mexico aboard the *Orpheus*. I could accomplish little else during the holidays. I was heartsick at the impending loss of all that I had built and I was sick physically as well; I suffered from gout, often the result of anxiety and stress, and I believed that a week away would help.

While we were on the cruise to Mexico, Jack Musiel, Westours' chief operating officer, called me by radiotelephone. He told me I had to get off the ship and come home. "Things are in terrible shape here, and getting worse by the minute."

My answer was that there was nothing I could do during the holiday season. No one was doing *any*thing. If I did come back, all I'd accomplish would be to wring my hands.

"But things are a mess, Chuck . . ."

I knew they were a mess, but my being there would not correct the situation. I appreciated his concern but did not leave the ship, even though all I could do was sit on the deck in the sun, my gouty foot elevated, and watch the all-too-few passengers stroll by. We had no alternative but to wait. And we might not hear — at all. It was either going to happen or not going to happen. If we were not bailed out, so be it. We had cut every corner possible. Kirk Lanterman had chopped personnel by one-third.

Everyone in the organization was apprehensive, but all we could do was wait it out.

Cruising aboard the *Orpheus* was not much consolation. The ship had berths for three hundred passengers; thirty of those berths were occupied by paying customers. I wondered how many passengers we might have had if Leisure International Tours had not gone bankrupt with $300,000 of our promotional money. We offered an interesting itinerary. The *Orpheus* was a good ship with an experienced and attentive crew — the Greeks know how to manage cruise ships. But as Sam Goldwyn said, ''People were staying away in droves.'' Sailing aboard the *Orpheus* was like being aboard a ghost ship. The week did little to help either my peace of mind or my gout.

We returned to Seattle only weeks before the million-dollar payment was due on the *West Star*. Spanish sellers of the ship had gotten wind of Westours' financial problems. They refused my request for a sixty-day extension but did grant me a thirty-day extension, saying that if on March first we did not have the money in hand, they would repossess the ship and sail her back to Spain.

Just twelve months earlier I had been riding high, at the pinnacle, it seemed, of my career. In January 1970 we had taken delivery of the *Cabo Izarra*, renamed the *West Star*, and sailed from Miami on a first-class cruise to the Caribbean, carrying the officers, board of directors, and entire staff of the ASTA organization as my guests. We served lobster, Beef Wellington, cherries jubilee. Drinks were on the house: the finest liqueurs, brandies, Scotches, Bourbons.

The ship was new. The program looked great. I had not the slightest inkling that a strike was impending. Now, just twelve months later, I faced the loss of my company.

At this point Holland-America sent one of its chief accountants to Seattle. He went through Westours' books with unrelenting thoroughness. And he wasn't pleased. Nor were his principals when he returned to Rotterdam and reported his findings. Then the transatlantic cables started to hum. There were days when I was on the phone to Holland-America at least once an hour during the working day. The Dutchmen were asking difficult questions for which they wanted straight answers — a game of intercontinental hardball was in progress. They questioned our calculations and wanted to know how we had reached our projections and how we could verify the information we had given them.

Business for Westours was not all that bad. Alaska bookings were up. We had enough cash to pay day-to-day expenses, but we were not gaining on that million-dollar ship payment; and with the first of March, Doomsday, fast approaching, we were dismally aware that we were about to lose the *West Star*. When this truth was finally acknowledged by me and the company officers, the only honorable action was to pick up the phone and tell the men in Rotterdam of our plight — that under no circumstances could I raise the March first payment, that in spite of this I still had a company that I wanted to keep alive, and that Van der Vorm and his associates were my best bet. I told them I was sending my attorney, Ted Wendells, to Holland so that negotiations could be completed and the contract for sale of a block of stock signed.

Two days later at four o'clock in the morning the telephone rang beside my bed. I had not slept — nearly out of my mind with worry, and suffering intensely from gout. Now Ted Wendells told me that Holland-America would not go through with the deal.

Ted Wendells is a splendid man with an extraordinary record of service during World War II, a man I had known and worked with many years.

I said, "You know what this means, don't you, Ted?"

"I know," he said.

"Once they repossess the *West Star*, everything goes. Westours will collapse."

He explained that Holland-America had simply lost interest when they realized that they would have to come up with a million dollars in cash within such a short time.

I said, "Ted, tell them I'm coming to Rotterdam to talk to them myself," And I hung up the phone.

At 4:30 in the morning I telephoned Jack Musiel and asked him to get me on the first airplane to Rotterdam. Jack protested, "I thought you were sick." I confirmed that I *was* but that I had to get to Holland as quickly as possible. I said that I didn't care what airline he put me on, but I needed two seats in first class in order to elevate "this damned foot of mine." The gout was killing me.

Jack made the flight arrangements and picked me up at 8:00 a.m. to take me to the airport. I was in a wheelchair and every movement was agony — the pain was so intense that my suit was wet with perspiration. The SAS flight to Denmark, the transfer at Copenhagen, and the continuation leg into Rotterdam seemed interminable. A car sent by Ted Wendells met me at the airport and whisked me to the hotel. Ted was there waiting for me. He told me the meeting with the Holland-America people was scheduled as soon as we could get to their offices. "They're waiting for us right now. We should leave as soon as you check into the hotel."

I said that he would have to tell them I needed at least an hour. I was exhausted. The gout was excruciating. I had not slept in two days and I had not had an evacuation in four days. I needed a shave, a bath, and a change of clothing to at least *look* halfway decent again. In my hotel room I proceeded to the first order of business: with my pocket knife I carved a rectal suppository from a cake of toilet soap and, using the warm water of the bidet, gave myself an unorthodox but effective enema. With my alimentary system functioning once again, I soaked in a hot tub, shaved, and donned a clean change of clothes. Then struggling onto my crutches, I hobbled out into the hallway and rode the elevator to the main floor where I met Ted Wendells in the lobby.

The Dutch possessed the one cruise-tour component that was vital to the future of Westours and which I had not been able to supply: large, efficient ships. They knew how to manage those ships economically and profitably. I was convinced that Westours' marketing experience could keep those ships full during the Alaska tourist season. With Holland-America's infusion of cash and their maritime skills, Westours would once again be a potent force in the world of tourism.

Van der Vorm had absented himself from the meeting, leaving negotiations to Ari Lels, one of Holland-America's vice presidents. A Holland-America financial man was also in the room. I got into high gear, pointing out the many reasons why Westours could be a highly profitable company — which time has proved entirely true.

They bought the idea. And they bought the company. But I was at their mercy and the terms were theirs. They offered me one dollar a share — a million dollars for a million shares which constituted control of the company. I balked at the price but was able to get only another twenty-five cents a share from them. Business is business and they were shrewd businessmen. I was against the wall and they were able to gain control of the company for just pennies on the dollar. I was desolated. But I saved Westours.

My alternative would have been to liquidate the company. We had assets — hotels, ships, buses, property. I believe that had I simply "sold out" I would have been better off financially than by agreeing to Holland-America's take over. But I was thinking only about Westours as a viable company if we could just get through this crisis. That was more important to me than the dollars I might receive through liquidation. I never thought at all about liquidation. Save the company, keep it alive — that was my goal. I lost it in order to save it. Had I decided differently there would have been no more people working for Westours. Who knows what would have happened in the industry? The decision that day was crucial to the future of many families.

The deal was struck during the forenoon, formalized initially by no more than a handshake between myself and Ari Lels. That same day Holland-America transferred one million dollars to the Westours account at Chase-Manhattan Bank. I telephoned Kirk Lanterman and instructed him to fly to New York and hand-carry a cashier's check from Chase bank to the banking institution used by the Spanish ship owners. I had to be sure there could be no mistake, that the mortgage on the *West Star* would be paid.

The entire transaction took place within the span of one working day. And I have never experienced such relief in my entire life. The weight of the world had been lifted from my shoulders. We had saved Westours. And I was to remain as president and chief executive officer.

A small miracle attended the signing of the papers that gave Holland-America control of Westours. I walked out of that office without crutches. The gout and all its agony were simply GONE. Ari Lels invited Ted Wendells and me to have dinner with him and some of his associates. We laughed, told jokes, had a wonderful time. I felt well for the first time in months. From that day on, I needed neither crutches nor medication to walk on the foot that had given me such misery. My mental state was so radically changed that my sense of physical well being changed with it. I was a new man, as though I had gone through some kind of rebirth.

Out The Door

I returned to Seattle from Rotterdam, prepared to adjust to my new circumstances, to put the past out of mind and get on with the business of creating and selling tours. Then I learned something — not all at once, but little by little. I learned that my "circumstances" were not what I had anticipated, that my title, "president and chief executive officer," meant nothing to the Dutch.

Also, the Hollanders had agreed to crew and maintain the ships: maintenance was their job, selling was mine. That didn't pan out, either. My nemesis, the *West Star*, was still the responsibility of Westours' marine department. At the end of the 1971 summer Alaska season, we put the vessel in a shipyard at Burrard Inlet in British Columbia for maintenance and repairs before sending her to the South Pacific. On her subsequent voyage to Fiji, she made it as far as Hawaii in a voyage marred by poor service, mechanical breakdowns, and failure of the air conditioning system. Jack Musiel — at the time, senior vice president of Westours — and I met her at the docks in Honolulu and immediately began fending off angry protests by disillusioned passengers. During the time required for further mechanical work in Honolulu, I felt obliged to assume the hotel expenses of those inconvenienced people. Some were so disgruntled that they abandoned the cruise entirely, and I flew them, first class, back to their mainland destinations — courtesy of Westours and Holland-America.

When the ship finally reached Fiji after suffering several breakdowns on the way, she was mechanically unfit for the job she had been sent to do. Ted Wendells, our vice president of administration, was on board to supervise the voyage. He telephoned me from Fiji and explained the situation — crew members were dispirited, the passengers furious. He remained in Fiji to do what he could to help people adjust their travel plans.

Completely out of patience, I telephoned Captain Nels van der Berg of Holland-America's maritime department in Rotterdam. I said: "Captain van der Berg, this is Mr. West. The *West Star* is broken down in Suva. I have just fired the marine superintendent and the chief engineer. The ship is now your problem. It will remain dead in the water until you send personnel to Suva to repair her and return her to service."

He replied: "Mr. Vest, you have just stuck a feather up my ass."

"Well, Nels," I responded, "remove it, put it in your hat, and wear it with pride. The ship is your responsibility from now on." As might be anticipated, my abrupt manner did little to endear me to Holland-America's top management.

Unfortunately, the *West Star* was not our only ship problem. The chartered *Orpheus* sailed back to her Greek owners at the end of the 1972 Alaska season, and once again we had too little ship capacity to support future Alaska tour sales. We were able to fill that void for the 1972 season by blocking space on Canadian Pacific Railways' *Princess Patricia* and Canadian National Railways' *Prince George*. Although these ships were old and had been in Inside Passage service many years, they were comfortable and well run. They would meet our needs for the 1972 season but were a makeshift solution to an ongoing problem.

Searching for an answer, I contacted Westours' former financial man, Ray Kusler, who had joined Princess Cruises (later to gain fame as the "Love Boat" company). Through Kusler, I got in touch with Stanley B. McDonald, president and founder of Princess Cruises. McDonald held charter rights to the *Princess Carla* and *Princess Italia*, two ships that were ideally suited to Westours' expanding needs. He and I negotiated an agreement whereby he would relinquish his charter rights to the two vessels in exchange for stock in Westours. This seemed to me a straight-forward business proposition that would give us the ships we needed and also put us in a position to acquire Princess Cruises.

I presented the idea to Holland-America management and was told we would discuss the proposal when Nico van der Vorm and his family visited Alaska that summer (1972). Van der Vorm was to be accompanied by Campbell Buchanan, the new president of Holland-America's North American division — Holland-America Cruises. Buchanan had already given my proposal his tentative approval; only Nico van der Vorm remained to be convinced.

When the Van der Vorms arrived that summer I escorted them on their first trip to Alaska. He headed a lovely family — I greatly admired his wife and children; and he, himself, was a polished European gentleman. I was delighted to squire these gracious people through my fabulous land.

All during our tour of Alaska I tried to prevail upon him to set aside time to discuss the Princes Cruises proposal. He kept putting me off and time was growing short; I had already made an appointment with Stan McDonald to tell him the outcome of my discussion with the Holland-America chairman. We needed those ships. On the last evening of our tour through Alaska, I was host at dinner to Van der Vorm and his family. I explained at dinner that I simply had to talk to him before he left the next morning. He finally agreed to an appointment later that night after he returned to the hotel. He said that he and Campbell Buchanan would be at my suite at 10:30 p.m.

I went to my rooms to wait. The agreed-upon hour came and went. There had been no call, no message, no indication at all that Van der Vorm would be late or unable to attend our meeting. At about 11:30 I gave it up and went to bed, leaving the front door to my suite unlocked, just in case. I was fast asleep when Van der Vorm and Buchanan knocked at the door, let themselves into my suite, and came into my bedroom. The time was 12:30, two hours after our appointed meeting. Lying in bed, I raised up on one elbow and explained that I had gone to bed and that the meeting would have to be the next day. I could not understand Van der Vorm: he was so polished in many ways, yet in this situation he had not even done me the courtesy of calling to let me know that he would be delayed. I could only conclude that in Europe codes for courtesy were related to status. Van der Vorm was the chairman: if he wanted to wake a subordinate in the middle of the night, that was his prerogative. But we were in Alaska now. And neither my Alaskan background nor my natural temperament had prepared me for my "subordinate" role.

At a later date Van der Vorm summoned several of his top people to a meeting in Seattle where the Princess Cruises proposal was discussed. I was not invited to attend — my "enthusiasm might prejudice those unacquainted with the proposition." I had argued that we needed space on the Princess ships and that we must either buy the space on a per-passenger basis or buy the company that provided that space. I favored outright ownership, believing that any other approach would simply help a possible competitor — Princess Cruises — establish a position in the Alaska *tour*ist trade.

Holland-America decided against the proposal and the results were predictable: Westours handed Princess Cruises the opening it needed to start an Alaska cruise-tour division of its own. Early the following spring, about March of 1972, after twenty years at Westours, Jack Musiel left the company to join Ray Kusler and Stanley McDonald at Princess Cruises where he became vice president of sales for Princess Tours, a division of McDonald's cruise operation. Here, as I had predicted, was a new and direct competitor of Westours.

All this was still in the future, however. At the time, my persistence in trying to persuade the Dutch to agree was regarded as just one more instance of my unmanageability.

Not long after the decision regarding Princess Cruises, a meeting was called in Fort Lauderdale, Florida — a strange meeting, indeed. Participating were three members of Westours' board of directors: Jack Musiel, Kirk Lanterman, and myself. Nico van der Vorm was also there. I was to chair the meeting and had prepared an agenda. I also brought a tape recorder to record the information from which the minutes would later be taken. When we sat down at the conference table, Van der Vorm took a chair on the opposite side of the room, some distance from the rest of us. This seemed odd but I shrugged it off, turned on the tape recorder, and opened the meeting.

Van der Vorm said, "Turn off the tape recorder."

I explained that we usually recorded the proceedings.

He simply repeated: "Turn it off." It was not a request.

I inquired who would take the notes.

"There aren't going to be any notes."

I pointed out that we would have no record of the meeting.

"We'll know what went on."

I invited him to join the group at the table. He declined; and since the meeting was obviously entirely in his hands, I invited him to take charge. He simply waved his hand in the air so I started through the agenda. As each new item came up for discussion, all heads snapped toward Van der Vorm; a nod or a shake of his head determined the amount of time spent on each subject. The meeting was a charade; little was discussed, nothing decided.

Obviously, *this* meeting was not the reason for our having been called to Fort Lauderdale. I suspected what the real reason was. A travel writer from New York had called me a day or so earlier to say that according to street gossip Holland-America was making important changes at Westours: "You are going to be kicked downstairs."

His news was confirmed later that day in a meeting attended by Van der Vorm, Buchanan, Musiel, Lanterman, and myself. I learned that Jack Musiel and Kirk Lanterman would be co-executive vice presidents of Westours. Buchanan would be chairman of the board, and a Hollander Arie van Tol would be sent from New York to act as a kind of in-house chairman, overseeing the Seattle operation — instructed, I'm sure, to see that the brash West complied with Holland-America policies and priorities. I had become a figurehead president.

Let's face it, I wasn't a "team player." I had offended Captain Nels van der Berg with my handling of the *West Star* matter after her unfortunate voyage to the South Pacific. I had offended Chairman Nico van der Vorm by asking him to leave my room in the middle of the night in Alaska. And I had not been able to mask my impatience with their decisions, particularly their decision to abandon negotiations with Stan McDonald of Princess Cruises.

Underneath the superficial differences in "style" among the American and Dutch personalities who formed the interface between Holland-America and Westours was a fundamental, deep-rooted disparity in European versus American ways. And this was nowhere represented more amusingly than in the relationship that developed between myself, an ex-Alaska bush pilot, and Arie van Tol, an ex-Holland-America financial advisor from New York.

To an outsider Westours may have given the impression of being a "laid-back" company. In terms of the casual rapport among employees and the company's informal dress codes (sport coats were as acceptable as suits), it *was* a laid-back company. However, it was also a vigorous, hard-charging work force. People knew their jobs and worked at those jobs with enthusiasm.

Into this unceremonious atmosphere came Arie van Tol, attired in an elegant Homburg hat, austere dark-blue suit, white shirt, blue-black polka dot tie — and manner to match. His clothes did not matter; his manner did.

Not long after his arrival in Seattle, I went to lunch one day with several people from Westours' accounting department. That afternoon Van Tol came into my office and explained that in the Holland-America organization the executives did not fraternize with the employees. It just wasn't done. Executives might have luncheon with other executives, but *never* with employees. In my usual diplomatic way, I explained that protocols which might be considered appropriate in Europe — or perhaps even in New York — were out of place in Seattle. And I reminded him that he was in Seattle now. We had no caste system here. He never did understand and the confrontations between us continued.

On entering the elevator:

VAN TOL. (*sotto voce* to WEST) "Now, Mr. Vest, I vill haff to enter the elevator first."

WEST. (full voice) "The hell you will!"

On entering a restaurant:

VAN TOL. "You understand, Mr. Vest, that I should precede you through the door."

WEST. "Arie, it doesn't make a damn who goes through the door first. Can't you get it through your head that there are no protocols once we're out of the office? Even *in* the office your silly little rules make no sense at all."

I could hardly believe what I was hearing, and with the top executive in the company worried about who went through doors first, it was tough to arrive at the big decisions: motorcoach purchases, disposal of large pieces of property in Alaska, whether to cancel or go through with plans to build new hotels. I had twenty-seven years' experience in these matters; Arie van Tol had none. As the months went by it became increasingly apparent that he and I were anathema to each other.

In spite of all this, the summer of 1972 ground to a reasonably profitable close. With the company again performing vigorously, I wanted more than ever to regain control. I went so far as to tell Nico van der Vorm: "Either let me buy my company back or fire me." He wanted to know where I would find the money to buy it. I reminded him that I had found *his* money when Westours had been in dire straits. I told him I would pay him one hundred percent profit on his investment. All I asked was a six-month option. His answer was, "No."

As the months went by, we continued to meet head-on over decisions which my experience in Alaska told me were right. Sometimes I felt that perhaps the best way to accomplish what was needed would be to recommend exactly the opposite of what I thought was the appropriate action, being sure that the Dutch would overrule me and out of pure contrariness do the right thing.

Everything I had touched was an abomination to them — even after I eventually left the company. I owned options on a plot of land at the intersection of Fourth and Harrison in the lower Queen Anne district of Seattle. I had planned to erect a building there to house our company offices. After Van der Vorm refused to sell Westours back to me, I asked him if Holland-America wanted the option on the Fourth and Harrison property. He declined, so I retained it and later made several hundred thousand dollars on its sale. I had offered the option to Holland-America for $25,000.

Westours, while still under my direction, had purchased (for $100,000 at five percent interest) land in Juneau for a hotel, a prime piece of property directly across Gastineau Channel from the city. Holland-America later gave up that property. Westours had also secured corner lots on the main street of Whitehorse and had arranged to eliminate an alley by replatting. This created an exceptionally valuable piece of land. We had already begun construction of a hotel on this plot; foundations were in place and work was under way. After Holland-America bought me out, they sold the property — and later had to purchase a Whitehorse hotel in a less desirable location for considerably more than would have been involved in the original plan.

All of these decisions were cumulative irritants in an ongoing confrontation, but there was one decision in particular that upset me greatly. In 1961 I had purchased, in my name, a piece of property of about five acres at Paradise Cove on Lynn Canal near Haines. Later I purchased another piece of about sixty-five acres adjacent to and north of the first piece in the name of Westours. I bought the property from Martin Madsen, a Haines resident. Marty and his wife, Ruby, were Alaska pioneers who had secured an original land grant for the property. I had an agreement with Marty that the sixty-five acres would never be subdivided but would be kept as a unit for Alaskan residents and future visitors to Alaska to enjoy. It was more than a written agreement; it was a solemn pact as far as I was concerned. I bought the land so that its unspoiled beauty would remain intact.

When Holland-America bought me out, I reminded them of the pledge I had made in the name of Westours. I asked that the new Westours' owners honor the commitment I had made. No soap — they wanted to sell that beautiful point of land to developers for subdivision into lots. They said that if I wanted it so badly, I could have it for $2,000 an acre. I didn't have $130,000 kicking around not doing anything, but I did offer to buy half the land if they would contribute the other half, and together we would donate the property to the State of Alaska as a perpetual park in the name of Westours. They would have none of it; the land was sold to a group of investors who have since subdivided it.

Marty Madsen is dead now; and what could have been Madsen Park, donated to Alaskans and Alaska visitors, is now off limits to the public. This has particular significance in Alaska where suitable waterfront property is limited. Although Alaska has a longer salt water coastline than the rest of America put together, relatively little of that coastline would be considered "beach" property. In so many areas, mountains rise straight from the water's edge, making the waterfront completely inaccessible.

The original five acres that I purchased from Marty has been retained in our family, and I have finally seen the culmination of a long wished for dream to build a real Alaska log cabin, which is now completed on Paradise Cove. The cabin provides a great deal of enjoyment for our family. It is my intent that the property be retained in perpetuity for the West family.

Meanwhile, employee morale at Westours sank lower and lower. What had once been a spirited group of people had developed a "what's the use" attitude. During January-February of 1973, middle-management Westours employees wrote, and almost all of them signed, a petition requesting that I be restored as chief executive officer of Westours. This petition was presented to Van der Vorm upon his arrival in Seattle for a corporate meeting. In another meeting called later in Van der Vorm's suite at the Washington Plaza Hotel, I was accused of having authored and sponsored the petition. I knew of the document but was not its instigator. It was prepared while I was on a promotion trip in the Southwest. At the meeting the Dutch told me that restoring me to my former position of complete responsibility for Westours was out of the question — my attitude toward Holland-America was not acceptable.

In the end our differences were too many and too great. They asked me to resign and retire completely. My contract called for Holland-America to buy the balance of my stock in Westours if I left the company for any reason. The tender they made me was $2.50 a share, the current market value of Westours' stock. I told them I would not resign. If they wanted me out of the way, the record must show that they had fired me. I told them I would not politely walk away from a difficult situation.

In a final attempt to resolve our differences, Van der Vorm made one more offer: they would allow me to remain as chairman emeritus of the board, enjoying a substantial salary until age sixty-five but having no official responsiblities. My response to this offer was not overrefined, and I was told that I could pick up my check the following day — Friday, February 23, 1973. Let it be said that I did not go gracefully.

I did sign a two-year "non-compete" agreement. Holland-America wanted me to sign either a five- or eight-year agreement, which at my age would have put me out of the Alaska tourist scene for life. Even Holland-America eventually agreed that these longer-term arrangements were not reasonable.

Coinciding with these events Holland-America took Arie van Tol back to New York and brought in Jack Musiel, making him president of Westours, a highly effective move on their part; not only did it give Westours an able man with twenty years' experience in Alaska travel, but it deprived Princess Tours of his services. Had Musiel remained at Princess Tours, that company would have developed into a far more formidable competitor to Westours than it did. The story goes that Musiel had been approached to become president of Westours some time before I received my ultimatum, in which case the Hollanders had secured their position before they ever approached me with their final offer.

On that last, bitter Friday Jack Musiel spent most of the day in Arie van Tol's former office, dictating letters to travel associates, customers, people in the travel industry — advising them that I was no longer with the company. A recipient of one of those letters said later: "West would have written those letters — certainly he should have been granted the opportunity to make his adieus with dignity."

That day Jack did not come into my office, just across the hall, to see me nor did I approach him. It was an uneasy and embarrassing standoff between two long-time friends. The situation was especially disconcerting to me, because I knew that Jack's reason for leaving Westours to go to Princess was in large part owing to his disenchantment with Holland-America policies.

And that day set the tone for future relations between the new Westours management and its former president. A letter went out from Westours to the American Society of Travel Agents asking that my name be removed from ASTA's roster. ASTA's reply was that my contributions had earned me "an honored position on their rolls for all time . . ."

I was flattered, too, by an episode that involved Continental Airlines.

The airline invited me to consult with them regarding tourism in Micronesia. When I responded by explaining the change in Westours' leadership and suggesting that the invitation should go to the new president, Jack Musiel, Continental's reply was unusually direct: "The invitation was to the man, not the company . . ." I was very pleased to accept that invitation.

Holland America had asked me to be out of my office at the end of the workday on Friday. My family was there — my wife, children, their spouses — to help me clean out my desk and remove the wall hangings and twenty-seven years of memorabilia, under the watchful eye of Kirk Lanterman, who remained after the close of the business day as uninvited "security monitor." We were a *family* — together — at a very emotional time. None of us will ever forget that evening!

Ironically, my departure coincided almost to the month with the coming to Alaska of large, modern cruise ships — the missing ingredient that had plagued me off and on for twenty Alaska tourist seasons and which ultimately led to my loss of Westours. In 1973 Westours supplemented its cruise berths with blocked space on the *Island Princess*, sister ship to the "Love Boat." In 1974 space on two Princess Cruises ships, the *Island Princess* and *The Spirit of London* (later renamed the *Sun Princess*), was reserved for Westours' cruise-tour customers. In 1975 Holland-America finally brought one of its own ships, the *Prinsendam*, to the Inside Passage. In years since, the finest vessels in Holland-America's fleet have sailed Alaska's Inside Passage and have been an integral part of Westours' cruise-tour itineraries. Not only did the modern ships substantially increase the amount of cruise space available to support cruise-tour sales, but they added a new dimension to Alaska tourism — the excitement and glamour of "world class" international cruising. Alaska tourism has exploded accordingly.

I never wrote a symphony or created any other kind of work of art. But I did create Westours, which meant far more to me than money. The money was a way to keep score, a system of measurement that had meaning in the marketplace but which did not express the full meaning of those twenty-seven years. From the days when I dipped up ice cream cones for the Eskimos on Kotzebue's Arctic Ocean beach and recruited off-duty San Francisco firemen to help me drive a convoy of second-hand Gray Line buses up the Alaska Highway . . . to the years when we searched around the world for just the right cruise ship, I had gotten used to making my ideas work, gotten used to winning. But I "bet the company" once too often, and I lost.

And my dream, my creation, made a lot of money for the people that I lost it to. Van der Vorm, himself, described Westours as a "jewel in the crown of Holland-America Cruises.'' My company profited Holland-America many, many millions of dollars. I expect that they appreciate Westours for that, but they will never appreciate Westours the way I did. I built it with my heart. And that's where it hurt.

Quite literally — that's where it hurt. A few months after my departure from Westours, the Continental Airlines consulting assignment took me to Micronesia. There, I found time to do some water skiing. The water was warm, the weather beautiful; I was having a wonderful time skimming around Truk Harbor until suddenly all my strength left me and I became acutely unwell — faint, giddy, about to lose consciousness. I dropped off the skis and the boat crew took me to the beach where I lay gasping and panting for breath.

I attributed my weakness to being out of condition and vowed to start exercising more. Later that summer while fishing with friends on the Rogue River in Oregon I experienced the same uneasy sensations — faintness, breathlessness. I had dived off the stern of our boat to swim ashore and, overcome by weakness, came perilously close to not making it. My heart was sending messages. But I wasn't listening.

Then several weeks later while returning from Mexico, I rushed with my luggage to make a plane change in Ontario, California. When I reached the airplane I was almost in a state of collapse. Finally, I acknowledged that I should see a doctor. In November of 1973 I entered Virginia Mason Clinic in Seattle and the following month underwent double by-pass surgery on the arteries of my heart. How fortunate I was to have departed from Holland America Westours! The animosity and antagonism in trying to cope with the Hollanders surely would have contributed further to my heart problems and might have cost me my life. Within weeks of the surgery I felt strong again.

Time heals. And in time I perceived that what happened between me and Holland America was unavoidable. I was outspoken, opinionated, independent. The Dutch were systematized, disciplined, controlled — accustomed to having subordinates follow direction explicitly. All my life I had made my own decisions and lived with the consequences. I did not fit the subordinate role, could not defer to authority, was unwilling to ask permission to make decisions. I suspect that these traits would have caused problems for me in *any* organization that I did not head myself. And when the philosophical and cultural differences between me and the Hollanders were mixed with this, the outcome was inevitable. As an organization grows larger, it relies less and less upon innovation and ideas and more and more upon decision by committee. I didn't fit the mold.

PART IV:

STARTING OVER

A Non-competitor Starts Over

Retire?

Unthinkable!

Some say I'll go to my grave waving tour brochures. And that may be an exaggeration. But I loved what I was doing. And I'm certainly not a quitter — though I had lost the great company I founded and was out on my rear.

Had I been ready to retire, I might have accepted Holland-America's offer of an annual stipend to enhance an empty title. I was 58 years old. I had lost my life's work. I had plenty of money and a beautiful home. Friends asked me why didn't I just quit, prune my roses, drive my boat around Puget Sound?

Why did I have to build another tour company? The answer was that I still wanted to be a part of Alaska tourism. I saw opportunities to do what had not been done before. I could have invested in tax-exempt bonds and been many dollars ahead of where I am right now. Instead, I have had the satisfaction of creating another enterprise that is widely respected in the travel industry.

But it wasn't easy. It was harder the second time around than it was the first. Looking back, I can see that I was probably foolish to risk it.

When I started Arctic Alaska Travel in 1946, I was a young man with only the vaguest idea of where I was headed or of how far I could go — or of where the opportunities would lie. I had no experience and no plan. Ideas developed arbitrarily from month to month, year to year. But in just twenty years my company grew from a one hundred dollar investment into a multi-million dollar corporation.

In 1973, when I started over again, I thought I knew exactly what needed to be done. I had the experience. I had the capital. I had a clear vision —

I thought — of the step-by-step plan that would build my new venture. But as it turned out, I was beginning another twenty-year trek into the unknown, a trek that has sometimes been discouraging and hard. If it had not been for the determination and support of my wife and family and of a few others who believed in me, we would not have been able to do what we did.

We have come full circle now. We've been successful, and we're proud of our success. The wealth of experience we acquired during those early years in Alaska proved to be invaluable. We knew the product. We recognized opportunities. We were able to move quickly and take advantage of those opportunities.

The day after I left Westours, my family gathered at our home on Seattle's Magnolia Bluff. Marguerite and our children told me they believed in me, that they were behind me if I wanted to start over.

I decided to plunge ahead.

I had signed a two-year non-compete agreement when I left Westours. I read the fine print very carefully. It said that I could do anything that did not compete with what Westours was doing. Westours did not operate retail travel agencies. I bought a retail travel agency, Magnolia Travel in Seattle, and renamed it West Travel. The agreement made no reference to what my children might or might not do. My daughters Ral, CarraLee and Barbara and my son Dick sold their stock in Westours and used the proceeds to start a small tour and bus company, Weslee Enterprises (Marguerite's maiden name was Lee).

Nor did the agreement refer to what an old friend and long-time business associate, Howard Hansen, might or might not do. Howard had been vice president of sales for Westours. He started and headed a second tour company, TravAlaska Tours.

All of these developments were under way within weeks of my departure from Holland America.

Alaska was vastly changed from the years when I built my own hotel accommodations out of old construction barracks and supplied my own cruise space by chartering a converted warship. Hotels were now available in almost all Alaska cities, and more and bigger cruise ships were on the way. I was no longer obliged to invest in hotels or ships in order to provide beds and berths for my tour passengers. But I did need to control my own ground transportation to move my own customers from airports, docks and railway stations. Otherwise, the new tour company I envisioned would depend upon the schedules, prices, quality control, and whims of Westours.

Again, I carefully read the fine print in my non-compete agreement.

Holland America had motorcoaches in Alaska, but not public carrier buses. The Dutch company operated under ICC *Special and Charter* authority that prohibited selling transportation except as part of a tour package. Holland America did not compete with bus companies that offered point-to-point transportation to any passenger who bought a ticket.

That was all the opening I needed. I left Weslee Enterprises to my children and the retail travel agency to the agency staff and set out to purchase a public-carrier bus company. At that time, Canadian Coachways, a subsidiary of Western Canadian Greyhound, ran scheduled service through the Yukon, connecting at the Alaska-Yukon border with Alaska Coachways, which continued on to Fairbanks.

While still at Westours, I had learned that Greyhound wanted to sell its Coachways divisions. In March of 1973, immediately upon leaving Westours, I went to Calgary with Howard Hansen to talk to Western Canadian Greyhound. We wanted the authority to carry passengers between Whitehorse and Fairbanks. We were not interested in the segment from Whitehorse south to Watson Lake near the British Columbia border.

Greyhound people assured me they could split their Yukon route. They would keep the Whitehorse-Watson Lake segment and sell me their public-carrier authority between Whitehorse and the Alaska border. They offered me a management contract for the summer of 1973, pending approval of the sale by the Yukon government.

We named our new company Alaska-Yukon Motorcoaches. We bought four used buses and painted them with our company colors. We hired drivers, ordered uniforms, established tariffs and schedules — and within four months after I had left Holland America Westours, we were carrying passengers from Whitehorse through the Yukon and Alaska to Fairbanks.

But we had underestimated government bureaucracy. Greyhound had erred in its earlier assurances that approval by Canadian authorities would amount to little more than administrative red tape. The Canadians insisted that we serve the longer route from the Alaska border all the way to the British Columbia border. They also insisted that we operate year around, summer *and* winter. They even asked that we post a million dollar bond guaranteeing that we would provide bus service to citizens of the Yukon Territory indefinitely, regardless of profit or loss. That was too much. We returned the buses, got our money back from Western Canadian Greyhound, and dissolved the company.

We did not lose money on the summer's venture. In fact, we made a little, and the Coachways exercise spurred our interest in applying for another bus route. At the time, there was no bus transportation connecting with the Alaska ferries at Haines. Alaska's big Marine Highway ships serve all major communities in Southeastern Alaska and also sail south to Seattle. Passengers arriving in Haines who wanted to see more of Alaska had two choices: they could bring their car on the ferry or they could hitchhike. A bus service from Haines to Anchorage would give them another alternative. In the fall of 1973 we applied for authority to serve that route.

Immediately, every bus company in Alaska jumped on me. My old company, Westours, led the hostile forces. They didn't want me in business. And judging from the strength of their opposition, the people at Holland America had finally acknowledged that I had come up with a valid idea. We were applying for public-carrier authority and because Westours did not operate under such authority, they did not have legal purview to oppose our application.

They made their way around this by buying McKinley Bus Lines and they opposed our application in the name of that carrier. But we persisted — we hired attorneys, applied for licenses, stated our case at hearings and waited for approvals.

Helping me through these legal battles was my long-time friend Ted Wendells, who had taken leave of absence from his law firm in 1970 to become Westours' in-house attorney and vice president of administration. Shortly after I went out the door at Westours, Holland America relieved Ted of his legal retainer. They thought he was too chummy with me. That certainly may have been the case. In any event, I again retained him as my attorney — an ethical, honest man with a wealth of experience. We balance each other very well, Ted and I. He is quiet and conservative. Every once in a while, he quietly and conservatively grabs me by the shirt tail and pulls me back on course.

It was during this period — November, 1973 — that I entered a hospital in Seattle for heart surgery. But I never considered dropping our new undertaking.

We won the route case and were awarded temporary authority to carry passengers between Haines and Anchorage. Now we had to prove ourselves by maintaining a dependable, scheduled service. We bought two 12-passenger Dodge maxi-vans. My son Charles drove one; Ken Kvale, a former Canadian Coachways driver, drove the other. The vans had no space for baggage so we bought used U-Haul trailers and towed the luggage behind the vans.

We had applied for permanent authority to carry passengers between Haines and Anchorage. This committed us to serve the route year round. In summer the Haines Highway across Chilkat Pass is spectacularly scenic. In winter it is fog-bound, snow-choked and dangerous. From Haines to Anchorage is 785 miles of misery — slush, snow, sleet and wind. Ken Kvale drove the route, and his loyalty never wavered.

I remember one blustery day in Anchorage. Ken and I loaded baggage into a trailer while two sleek Westours buses boarded passengers nearby. The Westours drivers laughed as we struggled with suitcases, fitting them into the clumsy trailer. I said to Ken, "Just *wait*. Just *wait!* They'll soon know we're around." Ken smiled and said, "I'm with you, Chuck."

We kept to our schedule and eventually were granted the permanent authority we sought. This was a significant first step in a long-range plan. Meanwhile, we had demonstrated that the winter service was unprofitable and were allowed to drop the winter run.

Our next requirement was a tour brochure, which led to yet another confrontation between lawyers.

A tour company's brochure is its heart and soul. It has no "product" besides its brochure. You can't walk up to an Alaska tour and kick the tires or slam the door and listen to it "clunk." A travel agent cannot sell your tours unless your brochure is in the agent's files.

My two-year forced absence from the tour business was to expire February 3, 1975, and while the Alaska visitor season does not begin until May, promotional work begins much earlier. Most Alaska tour operators released their summer tour catalogs to travel agents the preceding October.

We had to produce a brochure if we were to sell Alaska tours for the 1975 season. And we didn't have much time. I thought about that. The covenant I had signed specified that I could not re-enter the tour business. But it said nothing that prevented me from *preparing* to re-enter the tour business.

So we prepared. We decided that as long as we actually offered nothing for sale before February 3, 1975, we were in keeping with the terms of the agreement. We certainly could not impact Westours' business by simply printing, but not distributing, advertising brochures.

On the other hand, it might have appeared that we were jumping the gun.

Some months before the February date, a Westours employee happened to see our new brochure at the printing plant that both companies used to print their advertising materials. Holland America Westours knew it was my brochure — my picture was in it. And they were upset about that.

Jack Musiel, then president of Westours, called me, saying: "You are in violation of your non-compete agreement. You aren't to compete with us until after February 1975." I said, "Jack, the folder has been printed but it hasn't been distributed. We haven't sent it out to travel agents. No tours are available for sale. So if you think I'm competing, hire an attorney." The incident led to a short, though brisk, exchange of letters. No damages could be proved.

In February, when the non-compete period ended, we assembled our new organization: Weslee Enterprises was merged into West Travel Inc.; Alaska-

Yukon Motorcoaches became a wholly owned subsidiary of West Travel. TravAlaska Tours, a dba of West Travel, became Chuck West's new Alaska tour company. I became president of West Travel Inc. and of TravAlaska Tours. Howard Hansen continued as president of Alaska-Yukon Motorcoaches, assisted by our daughter CarraLee.

We sold the Magnolia district retail travel agency to UTravel, and we moved — in the fall of 1975 — into new, larger offices in the Fourth and Vine Building of downtown Seattle.

Our beginnings in Alaska were conservative the second time around.

Ken Kvale worked out of his home; his wife Janice took business calls in their kitchen. My son Dick, Alaska manager for the company, worked from a desk in the lobby of the Anchorage Holiday Inn. My daughter Ral managed our Fairbanks services. She worked without an office, helping clients with their travel plans when they arrived at the airport or hotels. The following year Dick rented an apartment across the street from the Anchorage Westward Hotel. The apartment doubled as an office from which he called on local travel agents and sold space on buses and tours.

Our biggest investment was in vans and buses. In the beginning we had only the two Dodge vans. With the start of our tour operation in 1975, we bought our first bus, a second-hand GMC 4104 that had been reconditioned by Greyhound to be used in Liberia. When the Liberian deal fell through, we bought the old rig for $17,500. Howard Hansen and Ken Kvale dubbed her "The African Queen." After running The Queen for seven years over the frost heaves and gravel of North Country highways, we sold her for $16,500. She didn't owe me a dime.

The next bus was a newer model. Then we bought another and another, each an improvement over the last. By 1984, AYMC had grown from two Dodge vans to sixty vans and motorcoaches, including new Le Mirage 46-passenger coaches from Prevost of Quebec. The most modern highway coaches in Alaska now belonged to Alaska-Yukon Motorcoaches. We gave our customers the best, though we were far from the biggest.

Buses need maintenance. Ironically, our coaches and vans were serviced in a shop owned by Westours, the same company that was fighting every new route we applied for. By spring of 1979 the Westours facility could no longer cope with the workload required by our growing fleet. We arranged for maintenance by still another competitor, Transportation Services. This didn't help. Our buses were last in line for repairs, and work was not always to our liking. We needed our own garage and service people and bought the Winnebago garage in Anchorage. It had been built originally by America Sightseeing for a bus garage and was ideally suited for our needs.

Applying for city sightseeing licenses also became a challenge. When I applied for my first sightseeing license — in Fairbanks in 1947 — I simply went down to City Hall and filled out a form. That was that. By the 1970s it wasn't so easy. We needed to find a city sightseeing niche not already served by other operators.

We focused on our ability to accommodate small tour groups, using vehicles smaller than standard sightseeing buses. We had already modified several Ford vans, converting them to 16-passenger vehicles that were ideal for small groups of travelers who wanted a custom-made tour. These vans provided our sightseeing niche; we obtained sightseeing authority in Fairbanks, Anchorage and Juneau because of our proficiency in handling smaller groups.

Later, when Norman Kneisel gave up his American Sightseeing franchise in Alaska, we acquired that franchise and added sightseeing in Juneau, Skagway and Ketchikan.

Then, after all this effort, federal deregulation of bus companies a year or two later made all the expensive route authorities and licenses meaningless. Now anyone could operate anywhere. We expanded accordingly.

At the same time that we were building an Alaska motorcoach tour network, we were also starting, in a small way, marine tours on Prince William Sound and the Inside Passage. In 1974 I had invested with a long-time friend, Brad Phillips, in the 49-passenger yacht *Glacier Queen.* Brad had been an Alaska state senator and an early employee of Arctic Alaska Tours.

During the late fifties and early sixties, he had run day-boat tours from Valdez to Columbia Glacier. His first boat, *Gypsy,* was destroyed by the 1964 Good Friday earthquake. This left the Alaska ferries as the only passenger service on Prince William Sound — one of the most beautiful spots on earth. *The Milepost,* Alaska's best guide book, describes Prince William Sound as being "equally as spectacular as Southeast Alaska's Inside Passage."

Bordered on the west by the Kenai Peninsula, on the north and east by jagged peaks of the Chugach Range, and on the south by a chain of protective islands, the sound encompasses fifteen thousand square miles of scenic wilderness. Long fingers of the sea penetrate glacier-decked mountains. Many species of wildlife — whales, porpoises, sea lions, seals, mountain goats, eagles, sea birds — delight the visitor.

Brad had supervised the design and construction of a new vessel at a Washington shipyard, and for eight years he ran marine tours across the Sound via Columbia Glacier, connecting with our motorcoaches at Valdez and Whittier.

Our partnership agreement included a "buy-sell" clause, and in 1978 he bought me out and built the larger, faster *Glacier Queen II*. Then in 1981 he sold everything to Westours. The venture that I had helped start now belonged to my competitor.

We did not feel comfortable depending upon Holland America Westours for space and service, so for three years, from 1983 through 1985, we chartered the *LuluBelle*, a sleek yacht owned by Fred Rodolf, an Alaska pilot and skipper.

The *LuluBelle* had two drawbacks: it carried only 49 passengers, and the name "Lulubelle" didn't project the Alaska identity we wanted. We talked to Fred about changing the name and suggested that he build a larger boat, but we were unable to agree.

This led to our decision to design and build a new yacht: the 99-ton, 149-passenger *Glacier Seas*, launched in April 1986. New fiberglass technology and a computer-augmented hull design allows faster cruising speeds and greater fuel economy than traditional boats. The ship is also equipped with bow thrusters that are particularly useful for maneuvering through icebergs near glaciers.

Other innovations include a separate lounge area on the upper deck that is served by a second public address system. This allowed us to narrate tours for foreign-speaking groups without interfering with tour commentary for English-speaking passengers on the main deck.

The faster, larger vessel helped us to expand our land-sea itineraries in south-central and interior Alaska. Tours from Anchorage linked Prince William Sound with motorcoach tours to Denali National Park and other points.

Our experience on Prince William Sound encouraged us to look more carefully at the Inside Passage. The name "Inside Passage" is a misnomer when applied to the sea-lanes of Southeastern Alaska. It suggests that what we call the "Inside Passage" is a single channel when, in truth, dozens of inside passages meander like rivers through the maze of islands, reefs and islets of the Alexander Archipelago.

The main navigation routes through this wonderland provide direct access to the larger communities. If your objective is to transport a barge-load of cargo from one city to another, this main-traveled marine highway is the way to go. But if you want to view the primeval Alaska wilderness — its fjords, glaciers, mountains, forests, waterfalls and wildlife — then Alaska's less-traveled waters will show you immeasurably more.

When John Muir and his Indian guides paddled a canoe up the Alaska Panhandle in the 1870s, they devoted most of their time to waters that are well outside today's main-traveled lanes. Muir's book *Travels in Alaska* drew the world's attention to the fabulous beauty of Alaska's coastal wilderness. But even today, more than a century later, Glacier Bay remains the only destination lying outside commercial waterways that is regularly visited by the major cruise lines. For the most part, the liners still follow the same routes used by the container ships and the tug-and-barge companies.

This is not to say that the main channel is not beautiful. Forest-mantled islands and snow-capped mountains are everywhere. But it's all tame compared with the up-close panorama of peaks, cliffs, glaciers and fjords that lies a few miles east of the main route.

Admittedly, many cruise passengers aren't terribly concerned about which route they take. The ships that cruise to Alaska are the same ships that cruise during winter in other parts of the world. Their focus is on the glamorous life at sea: nightclubs, discos, casinos, swimming pools, gourmet dining. For no small number of passengers, these Las Vegas-style luxuries are more important than the scenic vistas across the rail. On the other hand, the huge size of the mega-ships and their continuing round of on-board excitement insulates travelers from the majesty of the natural wilderness that surrounds them.

A hunch told me that a significant number of Alaska travelers were ready to exchange the blackjack tables, jacuzzis, and cocktail lounges for a closer look at Alaska as seen through the eyes of John Muir. I had long dreamed of sending day-boat tours through those parts of the Inside Passage that the big cruise ships seldom or never reach. To see these lesser-known areas required a vessel that hugged the shoreline, an impossible feat for a thousand-passenger liner.

In 1984 we chartered the 35-passenger yacht *Stephanie Ann* from Steve and Laura Bendixen. We renamed it *Sheltered Seas* and used it in daylight-only cruises for four summers.

Each year we experimented with the itinerary. For a while we went out to Sitka and up to Haines on Lynn Canal. Eventually, we settled on a route that starts in Ketchikan, allows two nights in Petersburg, and ends in Juneau, giving passengers four full days to explore 400 miles of Alaska's wilderness shoreline. The large cruise ships travel this distance, using the main sea lanes, in 18 to 20 hours — and half of those hours are at night. Yes, at night!

Unlike other ships that cruise in Alaska, the *Sheltered Seas* sails only in daytime. Passengers overnight at shoreside hotels and lodges. This blend of daylight cruising with overnight stops at ports of call provides a much closer view of villages, towns *and* scenery than is available from a large ship.

We take people into the very heart of John Muir country — utterly unchanged from what it was 100 years ago.

Tracy Arm cuts through mile-high coastal mountains 50 miles south of Juneau. At its head are two tidewater glaciers, but for many passengers the fjord's main interest is in the towering, glacier-scoured granite cliffs that rise straight from the sea. Lichens, moss, bushes and perfect little Christmas trees cling to the tiniest ledges and crevices. Waterfalls — like pencil-thin streaks of white yarn — cascade down hundreds, even thousands, of feet from the mist-shrouded heights above. Some have sliced deep clefts and ravines into the fjord's sheer walls. Others spread wide, sliding down enormous rocky faces.

Hardly more than a half mile wide for most of its 22-mile length, Tracy Arm is not favored by the big ships. Its narrow width is confining for navigation.

Ninety miles south of Tracy Arm is LeConte, North America's southernmost tidewater glacier, one of the most active ice rivers in Alaska. Each day LeConte dumps millions of tons of bergs into the sea. The floating ice provides a refuge from killer whales for seals and their newborn pups. The whales prefer to avoid the fjord's glacier-silted waters. Thousands of seals gather here in summer. Overhead, bald eagles and Arctic terns soar between sheer cliffs that frame LeConte's icy face, 4000 feet wide at its base. Because of the shallow bar at the fjord's mouth, only small ships can enter.

South of Petersburg is Wrangell Narrows, a 23-mile natural waterway dredged deep enough to serve small ships and fishing boats. Two islands, Mitkof and Kupreanof, press close on either side, making the narrows a particularly good area for spotting deer. A part of the channel's sightseeing interest is its intricate system of buoys and markers that guide ships through picturesque islands and rocky reefs. Sea lions use the buoys as resting spots.

These were the attractions that we offered our passengers, but we were limited by the size of the *Stephanie Ann-cum-Sheltered Seas*, which on longer voyages could carry no more than 30 passengers. We needed a larger boat to justify a larger marketing budget if we were to sell these cruises through travel agents across the country. But the Bendixens were reluctant to invest in a larger boat, and we were about ready to give up on the daylight cruises.

Then one day in 1987, Pete Donau from Glacier Bay Lodge came into the office and told us his company was replacing the dayboat *Thunder Bay* with a new catamaran. Maybe this was the boat we were looking for.

I flew to Glacier Bay and met with Captain Dan Blanchard. We took the boat out for a trial and learned that while it needed to be refurbished and modernized, its 16-knot cruising speed was enough to meet our Inside Passage sailing schedule. As a result, we leased the *Thunder Bay* with an option to buy and spent a half million dollars to refurbish it. The refurbishing was supervised by Blanchard, who joined our company and became an invaluable asset to us.

The capacity of the new *Sheltered Seas* more than doubled that of the *Stephanie Ann,* enough for us to justify additional marketing expenditures.

And that's all we needed: a larger boat and increased promotion. In 1988 we tripled the number of passengers carried in the preceding year.

Providing tourist services was only half the battle; finding customers was the other half. Our capacity in Alaska grew hand-in-hand with increased production by the sales arm in Seattle. To accommodate the growing Seattle staff — sales, tour counseling, reservations, documentation, accounting, administration — we moved to larger office space in 1977, and again in 1984.

In 1975 our brochure was 16 pages. The next year it was 20 pages. In 1980, it grew to 32 pages.

As the new enterprise continued to grow, I found myself needing another "Jack Musiel," someone to take charge of the day-to-day management of the company and, in 1980, Dean Weidner, Alaska Airlines vice president of planning, joined TravAlaska as executive vice president. He stayed until 1984, when he left to give full time to his growing real estate management firm.

My son, Richard G. West, replaced Dean. Dick had had a thorough grounding in the fundamentals of Alaska tourism. He had started in the travel business, at age 13, as a hotel bellboy. He had been a baggage handler, desk clerk, deckhand on a tour boat, sightseeing bus driver, and tour sales agent.

By 1984, our Alaska staff had grown to 75 employees. Our total staff, including the Seattle office, numbered more than 100.

Struggle

We were growing, but we weren't making any money. We were providing jobs. We were sending more and more travelers to Alaska. We were building a fine reputation in the travel industry. But we weren't making anything on it. We were surviving. We were getting by, breaking even. And that's all we were doing. Each year all the numbers in our financial statements grew larger, *except for the bottom line.* Each year our expansion costs offset increases in income.

The problem went much deeper than simply not making a profit. We were risking our capital without increasing our capital. The company's future demanded an ongoing investment in equipment and operations. Each year our growth was based on loans that bankers insisted be *personally* guaranteed by Marguerite and me. We were using family funds to underwrite company financing. We had no basis for optimism except for our deep-down faith in our experience, ability and integrity.

We faced horrendous competition from two giant companies that, between them, dominated the overwhelming preponderance of Alaska tourism. They were, and are, foreign-owned companies with enormous capital reserves and powerful political connections and lobbying clout. Our tour operations depended utterly upon the availability of cruise space on their ships to feed out motorcoaches. They didn't own us — but they controlled us. They controlled fares, travel agent commissions, discounts, and the flow of passengers in and out of Alaska.

We went along from year to year always with the uncomfortable knowledge that at any time our main source of business depended upon their whims. We controlled our destiny about as much as we controlled the weather. And even the weather was more predictable.

What kept us going? Faith kept us going — our faith in our ability to prevail, our faith in the idea that we could survive as an independent entity. We believed there was a bona fide need for an independent American tour company serving an American destination. We wanted to fill that need. We were honest. We were giving travelers a reliable service. We believed there ought to be a place for that. But no one owed it to us. We had to demonstrate our ability.

In retrospect, thinking back over my life, I recall so many situations — episodes — that profoundly altered the course of my fortunes, but that were often totally unpredictable, serendipitous. In 1987 one of these happenings came along: another giant cruise company announced that it would sail to Alaska.

The Italian cruise line, Sitmar, with North American headquarters in Los Angeles, was expanding its cruises from Mexico and the Caribbean to Alaska's Inside Passage. The implications for us were significant. Sitmar would be the third largest cruise line on the Inside Passage, and unlike Princess Cruises and Holland America the line did not have its own ground operation in Alaska. Sitmar would require shoreside services — transfers for its passengers, port city sightseeing, and extended tours throughout Alaska.

Three companies offered the motorcoach services that Sitmar would require. Two of them, Holland America Westours and Princess Cruises, were Sitmar competitiors. The third company was us.

Westours didn't even see us as a contender. It was inconceivable to them that the upstart Alaska Sightseeing would be awarded a shore excursion contract from a cruise line of Sitmar's size and prestige. But we showed them. We designed a comprehensive series of Alaska land tours. We developed shore excursions for each of Sitmar's Alaska ports of call. Dick West and our vice president of operations, Tim Jacox, escorted groups of Sitmar's senior executives through Alaska. They inspected our garage and equipment and traveled scenic highways from Anchorage to Denali, Fairbanks and Valdez. In turn, we cruised on their ships. They got to know us and we got to know them. We came to respect each other. And we won them over.

We asked for a three-year contract because gearing up for the Sitmar operation would require that we borrow almost a million dollars to buy and refurbish 24 additional motorcoaches. A million dollars was a very large sum for us. We would need three years to justify and amortize the investment. And we got what we asked for. We were awarded a ground services contract for the years 1988, '89 and '90. But once again our company investment had to be personally guaranteed by West-family funds. This was our only option if we were to move forward with this opportunity.

We bought and refurbished the motorcoaches, painted them with company colors, put them on the ferries to Alaska, and hired a maintenance manager just for Sitmar. It was exciting, not only for Dick and me, but for everyone in the company. We all had a strong sense of pride and achievement, a sense that we were assuming our place in Alaska tourism. A personal rapport had grown up between our people in Seattle and the staffs on Sitmar's vessels. We liked them and they liked us.

In 1988 Sitmar sent two ships to Alaska and we took care of their shore arrangements, all the while looking forward to 1989, when the Italian cruise line would increase its Alaska capacity to three ships, each carrying from 800 to 1,100 passengers.

Then one Saturday morning, on July 28, 1988, I received a phone call from Dick, who had flown to Ft. Lauderdale with Tim Jacox. They were scheduled to take part in preparatory meetings with Sitmar's national sales staff and senior executives aboard the cruise ship *FairWind*. Instead they heard the announcement that Sitmar had just been sold to Princess Cruises.

Dick called me. I was at home on Bainbridge Island across Puget Sound from Seattle. I had planned a day's outing aboard our family cabin cruiser with Mike Hickling, a ship's broker from London, and Ray Kusler, former financial vice president for Westours.

When the phone rang, I heard the startling news that Princess Cruises now owned Sitmar. I stood there talking to Dick — with a whirlwind of thoughts and questions racing through my mind. Princess had its own ground services in Alaska. Would there be a place for us in that operation? What would happen to our enlarged fleet of motorcoaches if it turned out that, indeed, there was not a place for us? What would happen to the three-year contract we were relying on to pay off the huge loan we had assumed to gear up for Sitmar's passengers?

Aboard the *FairWind,* Dick and Tim had been prepared to give a presentation to the Sitmar group. They were scratched from the agenda. It was a strange interlude. The world was on hold. They and the entire Sitmar staff were enjoying a luxury cruise through tropical waters to the Bahamas; and almost everyone aboard — Dick, Tim, and all of the Sitmar people, including regional sales managers and vice presidents — were wondering what their futures would bring. All of them shared a prevailing feeling of uneasiness, while surrounded by a festive cruise ship atmosphere.

For our people here at home, the announcement came as a disheartening jolt. So much hard work was about to go down the drain.

When Dick arrived back in Seattle, he and I huddled with David Chan, who had just joined the company as vice president of finance. What were our prospects? We had created a new fleet of motorcoaches and might have no place to use them. We had acquired an enormous debt and could foresee no sources of income to pay off that debt. We had been looking forward to the biggest earnings in the history of our company. Now we were looking at the biggest debt in the history of the company, with few prospects for paying it off unless Princess Cruises honored the Sitmar contract. If Princess chose not to, we had limited capital to fight a lawsuit that might drag on for years.

But there were encouraging signs. John Bland, Sitmar president, called me and pledged his support. ''I'm going to see that you are protected,'' he said.

I sat down and calculated what the loss of the Sitmar contract would cost us. The amount of our investment in motorcoaches and other advance preparations plus the amount of projected earnings from providing services for Sitmar passengers came to about $3 million, and this was what we asked to settle the contract. At first we were negotiating with Sitmar people, then with Princess Cruises. At the end of the negotiation we were talking to Ray Pedersen, president of Princess Tours, a division of Princess Cruises that headquarters in Seattle.

We negotiated and waited from July until the first week in October. Then one evening I received a phone call from Ray. At the time, we were holding an Alaska Sightseeing directors' meeting in a banquet room at Latitude 47, a restaurant on Lake Union in downtown Seattle. Ray said that he wanted to see me and came from his office to the restaurant where he, Dick, Tim and I adjourned to the privacy of the wheelhouse of our sightseeing boat, *Sheltered Seas,* moored at a nearby pier.

In the wheelhouse Ray handed me a check for $1,125,000. We shook hands, drank a champagne toast, and he left. That was that.

The settlement fell far short of the income we would have earned if Sitmar had not been sold and we had gone ahead with the ground services program we contracted for, but it did relieve us of our crushing debt burden. And with our limited cash reserves, we were in no position to fight an extended legal battle with a corporation as huge as Princess Cruises.

We could breathe again. But, in perspective, our circumstances had reverted to the conditions that had prevailed in past years. The increased earnings we had anticipated from the Sitmar contract were gone forever. Looking ahead, what were our prospects? We could see no justification to anticipate that our future financial position would improve over what it had been in the past. One thing I was sure of — we would never again jeopardize our future by placing ourselves in a spot where we must rely on another company's decisions. We must take time and develop our own niche. But where was that niche?

Immediately after we received the million-dollar Princess check, our new financial VP David Chan did a cash projection and informed us that, even with the extra funds in hand, we needed to cut our expenses. We went into an austerity program. We asked employees, including executives, to hold the line on salaries. At one of our meetings I made a statement to the staff: "We are in an extremely tough situation now, but when we get profitable I promise you that you will share in the bonuses." That's a promise Dick and I were later able to keep.

With these measures in place, we decided to forge ahead. We had enough faith in ourselves to move into larger office space. We decided we must bolster our sales division, and early in 1989 we engaged Thomas J. Bolger, former vice president of sales at Princess Tours, to head up a more aggressive sales program for us. He became our vice president of marketing and sales.

Then early in 1989 another of those serendipitous happenings came along. The oil tanker Exxon Valdez went aground on its way out to sea from Valdez on Prince William Sound. It is terribly ironic that the biggest ecological disaster in the history of Alaska turned into a financial boon for several players in the Alaska travel industry. VECO, the Exxon company responsible for the oil cleanup, immediately needed small ships to get the cleanup underway. Our sightseeing vessel, the *Glacier Seas*, just happened to be tied up in Valdez for the winter. VECO contracted for a six-week charter of the *Glacier Seas*, giving us unexpected income and easing our cash position.

VECO had asked us for a four-month charter. If we had accepted it we would have realized a huge increase in income; but we turned it down because we felt we had to keep faith with the travel agents across the country who had been booking clients all winter long on summer-season Prince William Sound cruises. As it turned out, Westours, which also operates Prince William Sound cruises, chartered its *Glacier Queen II* to VECO and arranged with us to carry Holland America passengers on the cross-sound route for the summer. This, too, helped our cash flow.

So, in less than a year, we had gone from looking forward to healthy profits to the prospect of sinking beneath unmanageable debt, and from there to an equitable settlement with Princess, and onward to two sources of unforeseen income as the result of an ecological disaster. Because of these events we found ourselves, in September of 1989, ready to take advantage of two more serendipitous happenings that would thrust our company in a new direction and into the special niche we had been searching for.

Building a Cruise Company

As the years went by, I had become more and more aware that most Alaska cruise passengers were not really experiencing Alaska.

Since 1973, the biggest change in Alaska tourism has been the increase in the number and size of cruise ships sailing the Inside Passage. In 1992, 27 liners sailed Alaska waters. Their combined capacities amounted to a season-long total of more than 300,000 berths. The impact of these passengers on the hamlets that serve as Alaska cruise ports was, and is, overwhelming.

Thad Poulson, editor-in-chief of the *Sitka Sentinel,* expressed it this way: "If you haven't seen a ship the size of the *Westerdam* towering over a . . . village, you haven't seen one of the most grotesque sights in tourism."

As many as five of these huge liners may call in Skagway in one day. They unload up to 1,500 cruise passengers each. Tourists outnumber the town's permanent population by a ratio of six to one. Rank upon rank of visitors, marching four abreast, swarm along a few blocks of sidewalks that were built to accommodate just two pedestrians at a time. Walking through this swarm of humanity, I am reminded more of Disneyland than I am of the old gold-rush town I used to know.

Alaska's enormous size is misleading in terms of its capacity to accommodate visitors. Its area is larger than the combined areas of all of the 15 states along the Atlantic Seaboard. The distance from Ketchikan to Nome is greater than the distance from Miami to Boston.

But except for Anchorage and Fairbanks, its towns are mere villages. The populations of all of its six cruise ports *combined* is less than 45,000. Even Juneau, Alaska's largest port and capital city, is a small town compared with most tourist cities around the world. The appeal of these frontier hamlets is cheapened by the overwhelming numbers of tourists they are being asked to accommodate.

The same kind of overcrowding burdens other Alaska destinations, including Denali National Park.

Was there anything we could do about this? The answer to that question was that in a small way we were already doing something about it. The marine sightseeing tours on the *Sheltered Seas* and *Glacier Seas* were taking visitors outside the main-traveled routes into immense wild regions that are as pristine today as they were hundreds of years ago. And our success beginning in 1988 with the new and larger *Sheltered Seas* encouraged us to explore other ideas.

Not since Alaska Steamship Company ceased passenger operations in 1954 had an American-owned firm offered a summer-long schedule of Inside Passage cruises from Seattle.

Government restrictions, often referred to as the ''Jones Act,'' prohibit foreign-owned ships from carrying passengers between two American ports. Because of these restrictions, Vancouver in British Columbia has become one of the world's major cruise ports. During summer a fleet of large liners, all foreign-owned, sail from Vancouver to Alaska. What a strange twist of irony that an old law designed to protect the American ship-building industry has given a Canadian city and foreign-owned cruise lines a virtual monopoly on cruises to an American destination for passengers who are mostly Americans!

Seattle is a better port for Alaska cruise departures than Vancouver, primarily because of better airline connections to other parts of the country.

If we initiated a Seattle-to-Alaska cruise, we would be an American company sailing from an American port to an American destination. We believed this would have strong appeal to American travelers.

But we needed a ship.

In 1988 we had learned that Alaska Boat Company, headed by Orion Shockley, wanted to sell the cruising yacht *Glacier Bay Explorer.* By spring of 1989 we had agreed on a price for the ship, based on a lease with an option to buy. But when the Exxon oil spill hit the southern islands of Prince William Sound, VECO bought the vessel, paying nearly twice the price we had negotiated. VECO used it as a hotel ship in Valdez during the summer of 1989 and then put it up for sale again.

Meanwhile, an opportunity for a new and different kind of cruise opened up when the National Park Service announced that it was increasing the number of small-ship entry permits into Glacier Bay. Permits had been rationed since 1979 in an effort to preserve the humpback whale habitat. At the same time that we were negotiating with VECO to buy the *Glacier Bay Explorer,* we learned that additional entry permits were available. Recognizing this as an opportunity, we conceived an idea for Glacier Bay yacht cruises from Juneau.

Within a few months all the pieces came together. We bought the ship, applied for Glacier Bay entry permits and postponed starting Inside Passage cruises from Seattle until some other year.

Our purchase agreement was not completed until December, 1989. This gave us only a few months to refurbish the vessel and implement a marketing program to sell 1990 cruises. We renamed the ship the *Spirit of Glacier Bay*. We spent almost $1 million in refurbishing and produced and distributed a brochure to travel agents nationwide. We soon discovered that our idea for a new kind of Glacier Bay cruise appealed to many Alaska travelers. It was a financial and operational success in its first year.

The *Spirit of Glacier Bay* is an ideal size for such cruises: large enough to support a national marketing campaign, small enough for the intimate, up-close kind of cruising that Glacier Bay ought to have. The ship carries 58 passengers. It has an observation lounge, a dining room, private facilities in all cabins, and plenty of outside deck space for viewing and photographing scenery and wildlife.

Traditionally, Glacier Bay sightseers had had two options. One was to sail aboard a large cruise liner that allowed up to six hours in the park as part of an Inside Passage cruise. The other was to fly to Glacier Bay from Juneau, transfer to Glacier Bay Lodge, and the next day transfer to a high-speed sightseeing boat that went up the bay's west arm and back, then transfer to the flight back to Juneau. Our cruise offered a more relaxed, leisurely trip that eliminated the transfer hassle and also gave travelers a better tour of park attractions.

We scheduled thrice-weekly sailings. The itinerary allows a full 24 hours in Glacier Bay. Passengers board the ship in Juneau and sail overnight through Icy Strait. They wake up the next morning at the face of Grand Pacific Glacier, deep inside the park. The ship also visits Johns Hopkins, Reid, Margerie, Toyat and Lamplugh Glaciers in the bay's west arm and Muir, McBride and Riggs Glaciers at the head of Muir Inlet in the east arm.

The *Spirit of Glacier Bay* is the only cruise ship that explores both arms of Glacier Bay — east and west. A park service naturalist who boards the ship at the park entrance lectures and answers questions about the region's wildlife and natural history.

When the English explorer George Vancouver surveyed the Inside Passage in 1794, Glacier Bay did not exist. Its entire present-day 65-mile length was filled with ice. Since then the glacier wall has retreated up several fjord-like inlets, leaving behind some of Alaska's grandest scenery and a vast unspoiled habitat for birds, seals, porpoises and whales.

More than a century ago John Muir described Glacier Bay as "a picture of icy wildness unspeakably pure and sublime." In 1925 the region was set aside as Glacier Bay National Monument. In 1980 it was enlarged to become Glacier Bay National Park, encompassing 5,200 square miles of pristine wilderness.

Aboard our cruises, travelers see a changing landscape as they sail the length of Glacier Bay's two main arms. Retreating glaciers during the past 200 years have created a back-through-time progression in the kinds of vegetation growing along the shoreline. Mature Stika spruce at the bay's entrance give way to transitional alder and willow, then to fireweed, brush and mosses. Finally, near the glacier faces, barren rock prevails, scoured clean by grinding ice.

Given these fabulous natural attractions and a suitable mini-cruise ship to explore them, we had launched another successful venture.

We were beginning to be known as an Alaska small-ship operator.

Seattle to Juneau — Juneau to Seattle.

Meanwhile, our idea for an American cruise from an American port to an American destination was still on hold. Our success with the Inside Passage daylight-only yacht tours and the Glacier Bay cruises encouraged us to go ahead. But the idea required another ship.

We were interested in the *Pacific Northwest Explorer* a vessel which, like the *Glacier Bay Explorer,* had been leased by now-bankrupt Exploration Cruise Lines. This ship, too, had been chartered by VECO. It came back on the market in the fall of 1989 after Prince William Sound cleanup efforts ceased for the winter.

We started negotiations for a lease-with-option-to-buy agreement with David Hartman, managing director of the Alaska Pacific Boat Company, and were close to an agreement when the partnerhsip owners received a cash offer from a Miami firm that intended to use it as a gambling boat off the Florida coast.

Once again we bided our time until we learned in August, 1990, that the Florida people had withdrawn their offer. We renewed negotiations and by the end of September had arrived at an agreement. We now faced another busy winter remodeling a ship and marketing a new kind of cruise.

By April of 1991, thanks again to Dan Blanchard and his crew, the 158-foot, 99.7-ton *Spirit of Alaska* (our new name for the *Pacific Northwest Explorer)* was ready. Built in 1980, the vessel has 40 cabins, a dining room, a sports deck and an observation lounge. It is the right size for the kind of Inside Passage cruising that we visualized — small enough to maneuver through the coves, narrows and fjords, large enough to give passengers comfortable overnight amenities.

Our belief in Seattle as an embarkation port for Inside Passage cruises was borne out by exceptionally strong sales. In the first year the cruise was booked to almost 100% capacity.

A listing of the ports and highlights of this cruise reads like a compre-hensive directory of Inside Passage attractions. Eight-day, seven night voyages sailed from Seattle to Ketchikan, Petersburg, Sitka and Juneau. Southbound voyages called at the same ports in reverse order. The ship also sailed through Washington State's San Juan Islands and Desolation Sound in the Canadian part of the Inside Passage. The route transited Wrangell Narrows and Peril Strait, and visited Misty Fjords National Monument, LeConte Glacier Fjord and Glacier Bay.

The one-way itinerary, beginning or ending in Alaska, allowed travel planners to combine the cruise with an ongoing tour to other parts of Alaska: Denali National Park, Anchorage, Fairbanks, the high Arctic, and other points.

One of our biggest hurdles in acquiring the *Spirit of Alaska* was financing a mandatory Federal Maritime Communications Commission bond required of all vessels carrying 50 or more overnight passengers. We needed $750,000 in cash. This stretched our finances, but we managed it.

From time to time as our company continued to grow, the company name also changed and "grew," keeping pace with our expansion into new ventures. We had started as Alaska-Yukon Motorcoaches and TravAlaska Tours. For a few years we offered sightseeing under the name Alaska Sightseeing Tours. These two names were merged to become Alaska Sightseeing Tours/TravAlaska.

As we continued to acquire new ships, we expanded our operations from Alaska into the Pacific Northwest, offering spring and fall cruises from Seattle to the San Juan Islands and British Columbia. In 1991 we introduced a new Columbia/Snake River cruise from Portland. We needed a company name that encompassed those regions. The name we selected was Alaska Sightseeing/Cruise West. Our company logo is an adaptation of the logo we used when I started my first Alaska cruise line in the 1950s: a white polar bear in a circle of blue, instead of a triangle of blue (it appears on the dust jacket of this book).

Finally in the mid-1990s we moved entirely to the name Cruise West. This name — which, like Holland America Westours, still contains my family name — now proudly covers all of our company's public operations, from Alaska ground operations by motorcoach and tour bus to cruise routes that span the entire Pacific Rim, from the west coast of North America to the Far East and the South Pacific. Plus Cruise West still offers a wider range of cruise routes, and wider net of ports visited, than any other operator in Alaska, including the huge multinationals. But I'm getting a bit ahead of myself.

A year after we acquired the *Spirit of Alaska*, still another ship became available. Anchored at Bainbridge Island, across Puget Sound from Seattle, was a mini-cruise ship named the *Columbia*. This vessel had also been purchased by VECO to help with the oil-spill cleanup. Its size was a perfect match for the *Spirit of Alaska*. And by now we were ready for it.

The *Columbia* had returned from Alaska in the fall of 1990. At that time we were not interested, but a year later, with the success of the *Spirit of Alaska* cruises from Seattle behind us, we were encouraged to go ahead.

A boat is valued only by what it will earn. Tied up at a pier, it's worthless, a liability that can sit idle for only so many years before it's scrapped. The *Columbia* had been idle for quite a while. The oil spill cleanup gave it a new life, but now it was tied up at a pier again.

The *Columbia* has 42 outside cabins, all with private facilities, on three passenger decks. Public areas include a dining room, fore and aft outside decks and an observation lounge.

We negotiated with VECO, and for the third winter in a row Dan Blanchard's crew was remodeling a small cruise ship. In April of 1992, the 166-foot, 96-ton *Columbia*, renamed the *Spirit of Discovery*, joined the *Spirit of Alaska*, sailing out of Seattle to Juneau.

Then, in the summer of 1992, we learned that yet another small ship was up for sale, the 101-passenger *Victorian Empress*, owned by American Heritage Cruises: 96 tons, 192 feet long, 49 cabins.

Our new Inside Passage cruise had been so successful that we thought there might be room for a third ship on the Seattle-Alaska route. On the other hand, the asking price for the Victorian Empress was more than we thought we could afford. A ship is worth only what it will earn, and our projections indicated that the vessel would not earn enough to justify paying what American Heritage was asking.

Purchase negotiations began that summer and for several months we went back and forth across the country. In October Marguerite and I flew to Quebec and cruised the Saguenay River and St. Lawrence Seaway on the ship. We feel in love with the boat. Although relatively new, built in 1984, its design and décor are evocative of Victorian-era steamboats. Appointments are lavish for a small vessel. Lots of brass and mahogany.

But with winter approaching, we found ourselves caught in a time squeeze. There was a risk that negotiations would not be completed before locks on the St. Lawrence River closed. We needed seven weeks to bring the ship 8,400 miles down the Atlantic coast, through the Panama Canal and up the West Coast to Puget Sound. With all the other uncertainties that beset us, we could not afford to risk the additional uncertainty of waiting until spring when the St. Lawrence Seaway reopened.

We must conclude the deal now — and more than a million dollars stood between the price we were offering and the price American Heritage was asking.

In each of the four preceding years, we had purchased a new ship that was larger than its predecessor. Now we were looking at a ship that would require a larger investment than all of the other four combined. We had undergone several years of rapid growth. We had been successful. It appeared, based on past years' sales figures, that there was room for a third ship on our Seattle-to-Juneau cruises. On the other hand, how close were we to the saturation point for these cruises? How much more growth would the market support? These risks were imponderables.

And there was yet another element complicating the negotiation. We had proved — not only to ourselves but to the rest of the travel industry — that our Inside Passage cruises from Seattle were a hot item. If we did not go through with our purchase of the *Victorian Empress*, it was possible that someone else might buy the ship and put it on the Inside Passage in direct competition with the route that we had pioneered.

The *Victorian Empress* was the last remaining "T-category" vessel available in North America: the only remaining vessel that complied with Coast Guard requirements for cruising between Seattle and Juneau. These requirements are that the ship must be an American flag vessel (built in the United States) and it must be under 100 tons to comply with Coast Guard regulations for crewing and other rules.

Because of the inflation in construction costs, it would not be possible for us to build a new ship. We must buy this one or let it go and possibly watch someone else use it to compete against us.

But a ship is worth only what it will earn.

With these thoughts in mind and the closing of the St. Lawrence Seaway less than six weeks away, I picked up the phone on Thanksgiving Day in Borrego Springs (where Marguerite and I were spending a few weeks) and called Bob Clark, one of the owners of American Heritage cruises, in Quebec.

I explained the urgency of concluding the deal before winter. I raised our offering price, but not up to his asking price — and he wouldn't budge. I told him that this was our final offer and that we must have an answer by the Monday following Thanksgiving or we would withdraw the offer.

In the end we were successful. We negotiated a purchase agreement and brought the *Victorian Empress* through the locks before winter closed in. We renamed the ship the *Spirit of '98* and offered Alaska Inside Passage cruises beginning in the spring of 1993.

In 1994 Cruise West began offering a fourth West Coast destination: the lush and lovely California Wine Country. In the Napa and Sonoma Valleys a sunny climate and rich volcanic soil meet lifestyle, art, architecture and gardens to form one of the most congenial and creative areas on earth. Sailing up the Napa River right from San Francisco's central waterfront, we found ourselves introducing our guests to century-old caverns stuffed to the ceiling with fine champagne, with lunches al fresco served among olive groves and vineyards, and sampling fine sparkling wine on the terrace of a French-inspired chateau.

Our fleet didn't expand for a few years, until we saw the *Sea Spirit* at anchor in Elliott Bay. This 217-foot beauty was for sale, and we couldn't resist. The newly rechristened *Spirit of Endeavour* became our 102-guest flagship, allowing us to expand our Alaska offerings yet again in the summer of 1998. That winter, Cruise West also for the first time cruised south of the border to Mexico's Sea of Cortés.

To people who only know Mexico from the news, or from exposure to the popular large resorts of the Mexican Riviera and Cancún, the Sea of Cortés is an amazing surprise. Along the Baja Peninsula, the almost 900-mile expanse of rugged desert shoreline backed by steep mountains is barely populated, in many places roadless. Offshore, pristine islands blanketed by a veritable forest of tangled cactus and succulent plants invite hiking, beachcombing, and swimming in the crystal-clear water. This warm-weather destination introduced our guests to Zodiac-like inflatable craft operation — step from your ship to the inflatable and zip to a wilderness beach, there to swim, snorkel and kayak. Inflatables proved so popular that we have introduced them on several Alaskan routes as well as all our other warm-weather destinations.

By the late 1990s I had turned over hands-on management of Cruise West to my son, Dick West, including voting control of the company. Dick started in the tourism business as a teenager handling baggage at one of our hotels in Alaska, and rose through decades of on-the-job experience. Now, as Chairman and CEO of Cruise West, Dick has capably led the company into its present — with some notable bumps along the way — 9/11, anyone? Adding to the management strength is Jeff Krida, formerly of the Delta Queen Steamboat Line, who has served as President and COO since 2000.

In 2000, the American economy, and especially that of the Pacific Northwest, was booming. The stock market was soaring high, dotcom businesses were mushrooming overnight, and everything looked rosy.

It seemed a great time to get international. A small luxury cruise ship was for sale in Singapore. Originally built in an Italian shipyard as the

Renaissance V, the vessel was then being operated as the *MegaStar Sagittarius*, offering gambling junkets in Singapore and Malaysian waters. High rollers would step on board for a night's play, including a stateroom, and return to port the next day rolling in cash (or regrets!).

We bought the ship and renamed her the *Spirit of Oceanus*, after the Greek god of the seas. This was Cruise West's first non-U.S.-flagged vessel, registered in the Bahamas, with an international crew and American cruise staff. She is suitable for cruising in all seas, and we set up itineraries in Southeast Asia — Japan — the Russian Far North, Alaska, and the South Pacific. Beginning late April, 2001, the *Spirit of Oceanus* sailed from Bangkok, Thailand on an ambitious itinerary via Vietnam, China, Japan, and Russia to Alaska's Aleutian Islands and the Inside Passage.

2001 turned out to be an iffy year to start such an ambitious operation. The stock market slowdown commenced, and then the events of 9/11 hit the entire world's travel industry for a loop. So for several years Cruise West restricted the *Spirit of Oceanus*' operation to Alaska, our core market, where she proved very popular at unique and far-ranging itineraries. The "Coastal Odyssey" ventured from Vancouver to Anchorage and back, with Zodiac excursions in remote bays and rocky outcrops. Even more adventurous was the "Voyage to the Bering Sea," an expedition-style voyage of exploration from Anchorage to Kodiak, the Alaska Peninsula, the Aleutians, and the remote musk-ox inhabited islands of the Alaska Maritime National Wildlife Refuge. This itinerary even visited Chukchi villages in the Russian Far North, and Yu'pik villages in remote Alaska.

In 2001, Cruise West also inaugurated its first partnership cruises with a family-owned company in Costa Rica who ably operated the *Pacific Explorer*. Sailing in Costa Rica and Panama waters, guests could step ashore by Zodiac at a coconut palm-lined island beach, or a remote coastal wildlife refuge teeming with chattering monkeys. Operating in such tempting tropical waters whetted our appetite for more.

As I write in 2005, the global travel economy is thriving, and Cruise West's *Spirit of Oceanus* plans to revive her cruises to the far-flung corners of the Pacific Rim, from Tahiti in the South Pacific to the Inland Sea of Japan. While we will always retain our heritage in Alaska very close to our hearts, small-ship cruising — particularly our style of small-ship cruising — can operate practically anywhere on the planet!

The Future of Alaska

The first Alaskan port of call for most northbound Inside Passage cruisers is Ketchikan, just north of the Alaska/B.C. border. In the downtown core, the buildings of this old fishing and logging town are just three to four stories high. From the facades along the waterfront it's only about two or three hundred feet across Front Street and a broad wharf to the bollards where the big cruise ships tie up, sometimes two or three at a time.

From the dock up, these cruise ships tower thirteen stories or more, each a thousand feet long. Right next to a three-story town. That's quite a sight, to see these floating skyscrapers blocking the view of Tongass Narrows from the town. And as thousands of passengers pour into the streets, to find some of the same shops they might have seen in St. Thomas, or to buy souvenirs made in China, it's quite clear that mass-market tourism has made quite an impact on Alaska. Just what kind of impact?

I was privileged to be in at the beginning of Alaska's postwar tourism industry. The tour and cruise patterns we developed in the 1940s and '50s became a template that shaped an industry which now challenges timber and fishing as major players in the Alaska economy.

I was privileged again — in the 1970s — to start over and create a second company, one that carved its own unique niche in Alaska tourism (although it seemed more of a struggle than a privilege at the time). Cruise West is today Alaska's — and North America's — largest small-ship cruise line. We're still American owned, and family operated.

I've been successful, and I confess that it feels good. But I measure my success less in terms of dollars than in the quality of the experience we have provided to people seeking out the wonders of Alaska. We fulfilled their dreams, and sent our guests home with memories to cherish for a lifetime. That's where my greater satisfaction lies: our reward derives from watching thousands of travelers come closer to Alaska's still-untouched wilderness than is possible any other way.

That's part of my frustration, too. Too many travelers to Alaska today don't actually get an individual, high-quality experience. They don't make a personal connection with Alaska, or any Alaskan people. Tens — hundreds — of thousands come to Alaska on a foreign-owned mega-cruise liner, served by Filipino or Indonesian stewards. At the pier in Alaskan ports, they step onto a long line of motorcoaches, all owned by the same foreign-owned company that owns the cruise ship. In Anchorage or Fairbanks, Denali National Park or Kenai, they stay in one of a hotel chain, also owned ditto.

A recent headline in the Juneau Empire asked "Tourism: Is Juneau ready for a million cruise passengers?" Small-ship cruise companies combined, Cruise West included, bring about 12,000 guests per year to Alaska, at 80 to 100 guests per voyage. That's scale, that's intimacy, that's a great perspective on a great land. The rest of those cruise multitudes arrive on foreign cruise ships.

At this point in the early 21st century, a few vast multinational businesses dominate the Alaska travel business. Carnival Corporation & PLC alone is the parent company to Carnival Cruise Line, Holland America, Princess Cruises, P&O Cruises, Seabourn and Windstar — 12 cruise "brands" in all. Its total passenger capacity worldwide is 113,296 - at a time! Another big player is Norwegian Cruise Line — owned by Star Cruises of Hong Kong.

These businesses do their very best to achieve what economists call vertical integration — they want to control the business from booking to delivery — the cruise ships, motorcoaches, tour buses, railroad cars, and hotels. The profits leave Alaska.

And by being owned or registered overseas, very few of their business operations in Alaska pay federal taxes. In fact, if it were not for some ground-based units such as Princess Hotels, the multinationals would not pay any federal taxes at all. They just haven't found a way (yet) to claim that, say, the Denali Princess Lodge is actually located in the Bahamas.

The impact of industrial tourism is very high in many ways. In the summer, hundreds of floatplanes a day fly over Juneau's residential Mendenhall Valley on 'flightseeing' excursions for cruise ship passengers, or along the shores of Ketchikan's Revillagigedo Island. Fairly low, fairly loud. Juneau, Skagway and Ketchikan in particular are affected in this way. Small towns get pressure to build more infrastructure — bigger docks, bigger wharves. As the most popular ports get overcrowded, the cruise ships are always seeking new places. A 1,000-passenger ship may visit the 3,000-population village of Wrangell, with predictable results. The only people you'll pass on the street are fellow tourists.

Quite a few Alaskans are getting upset at how industrial tourism is changing their lives, their landscape, their state. A few years ago Sitka citizens voted against a greatly expanded cruise ship dock project — it would have simply led to huge new showers of unwanted tourists crowding their streets. Nearly every year proposals arise in various port cities and even the state legislature to impose head or per capita taxes on cruise ship passenger arrivals. The most recent proposal was $50 per person. Now let's see... Today's large ships can be 2,000 guests easily. Times $50 each. Per week. That's — $100,000 per ship, per week! Each time this happens, the cruise lines gear up their lobbying and public relations teams. But I fear it's going to be a long fight.

I've presented this brief sketch of current conditions because Alaska did not have to be like that. And it doesn't have to be like that today, as far as an individual's travel experience goes. Small entrepreneurs all over Alaska are emerging with ideas for the future, just as I did as a young man. Upscale fishing lodges in the wilderness, and bed & breakfast inns in the towns. Jetboat runners, and raft operators. Tours by helicopter and floatplane, kayak and canoe, horseback and foot are everywhere available — for those who seek them.

These 'best of Alaska' experiences are everywhere — they're just not so easy to find. The closest any passenger on a large cruise ship will come to them is on a shore excursion in port. Which is always at extra expense, of course — not enough profit, or volume, in it for the cruise line to care much about.

I think an ideal vacation experience in Alaska incorporates the best of the land and sea. Book yourself a seven-night small-ship cruise on one of Cruise West's small ships. Zodiac into remote coves, spend a night at anchor under snow-capped cliffs, negotiate deep into glacier ice to the front of a glacier. Then reach out, perhaps with just your family, to one of the myriad small operators who want to host you in the wilderness, and show you their version of the "real Alaska." Fly to a lakeside lodge, a hundred miles from Anchorage, and commune with bears fishing for salmon below. Small scale and personal encounters with Alaskans and their landscape are exactly the right way to truly experience the grandeur of the Great Land.

Looking ahead for my children and their kids — what do I want for them? More than anything else, I want them to understand that personal integrity is the most important element in the conduct of one's business. And I want them to know how important it is to retain one's self-respect and the respect of those in the business community.

I hope that my children, grandchildren and great grandchildren will share my love for Alaska, which has dominated my life for the last sixty years.

I am grateful for all of life's blessings.

Awards

Almost exactly fifty years after flying "The Hump" into China during World War II, I received a letter from the United States Air Force which stated, ". . . the Secretary of the Air Force has granted you special award of the Distinguished Flying Cross and Air Medal for meritorious achievement while participating in aerial flight as a member of the Army Air Force China National Aviation Corporation ATC group. These prestigious decorations recognize your gallant efforts while participating in many hours of operational flight over the dangerous and difficult Assam-China air routes, flying day and night missions at high altitudes over impassable, mountain terrain through areas of extremely treacherous weather conditions." The letter and awards were unexpected after all these years, but, needless to say, I am thrilled to have received this recognition.

In 1988 at the American Society of Travel Agents' World Congress in Budapest, I was inducted into ASTA's Travel Hall of Fame, the highest honor the travel industry can bestow. The award was presented in recognition of my "contribution to the tourist and travel industry, particularly in Alaska." I am understandably proud to be listed among other Travel Hall of Fame members, including such names as Juan Trippe, Neil Armstrong, Lowell Thomas, Walt Disney, Edward Carlson and Sir Edmund Hillary.

In 1970 I received the Golden Plate from the American Academy of Achievement. It is awarded to "America's Captains of Achievement, representing the many who excel in the great fields of endeavor."

In 1976 I received ASTA's Joseph W. Rosenbluth Award, which honors "the travel agent who has made the greatest contribution to the travel industry and whose outstanding influence and professional activity have advanced the status of the travel agency industry."

In 1991 I was named to the Alaska Business Hall of Fame.

In 1991 the Travel Industry Association of America presented its Travel

Industry Hall of Leaders Award, its highest honor and tribute, for my "outstanding leadership and significant contribution to the recognition, growth and advancement of the United States travel industry."

In 1992 the International Federation of Women's Travel Organizations presented me with its Berger-Sullivan Tourism Award in recognition of my "outstanding and ongoing contribution to worldwide travel and tourism."

Through the years, the Alaska Visitors Association has presented me with many awards including its North Star Award.

An Afterword

I would like to believe that I have been more than just plain lucky in my endeavors, that through the years I have developed sound ideas and business practices, that I have shown good judgment and followed an honorable ethical code. Here are my thoughts on practices and policies that have contributed to the success of our undertakings.

Management — Some businesses survive in spite of their management; some move ahead because of it.

Our acquisition of the *Thunder Bay* in 1987 and our introduction of expanded *Sheltered Seas* Inside Passage Yacht Tours in 1988 coincided with the gathering of a management group which I believe surpassed the old Westours in its innovative ability to work together and get the job done.

— Richard G. West, my son, became executive vice president in 1984, and as the years went by took over more and more of the management of the company. In 1992 he became president and chief executive officer. In 2005 he is chairman and chief executive officer (and owns a majority stake in the company).

— Dan Blanchard also joined us in 1987 to head our new marine division. He had been the former captain of the *Thunder Bay*. His experience, not only in operating ships but also in renovating and remodeling them, has been invaluable to us.

— John Kreilkamp, formerly station manager for Cape Smythe Air in Nome, became our director of sales in Anchorage in 1987, later vice president of Alaska operations.

— Tim Jacox, who joined the company in 1979, moved up through different positions to become vice president of operations in 1987.

— David Chan moved from Arthur Young, an international CPA firm, to become our vice president of finance.

A few years later, in the mid 1990s, Tim, Dan and David were all instrumental in founding American Safari Cruises, a luxury yacht operation that operates in Alaska's Inside Passage.

Time passes and faces change, but in 2005, Cruise West and its predecessors have been in operation for 32 years. Today's Cruise West is led by Dick West and president Jeff Krida, who came to us from Delta Queen Steamboat Company. We have a strong team based in Seattle and Anchorage that strives to provide our guests with the very highest quality experience possible. Thanks to the diligence and wisdom of our management people and their ability to work together cooperatively, we have made our way through a maze of change to where we are today. We have become a real company family.

The Six Cs — Through the years, I have sought to minimize entrepreneurial risk by evolving a set of standards that I feel must be in place before a new travel product can be successful.

The biggest risks come with the introduction of a new, untested idea. Our company's success is based almost entirely on travel products that were new and untested when we started them. These included the *Sheltered Seas* daylight Inside Passage cruises, the Glacier Bay cruises from Juneau, and the Inside Passage cruises from Seattle. With the introduction of each of these new products, we moved into unexplored territory. I have given a name to the set of standards that must be in place before introducing new ideas. The name is "The Six Cs." Here is an example of how they applied when we planned our new Glacier Bay cruises from Juneau in 1990.

1) *Concept:* first we must have an idea for a new kind of service, something not yet offered that will appeal to Alaska travelers. In this instance, our idea was a way to see Glacier Bay that would be more comprehensive and convenient than any other cruise or sightseeing excursion.

2) *Chance:* concept alone is not enough. We must also be a little bit lucky. In Glacier Bay we were fortunate that the opportunity to purchase the *Glacier Bay Explorer* came along at a time when we were ready to expand. It was also fortuitous that the National Park Service coincidentally opened Glacier Bay entry permits for bid and that we were able to

negotiate three permits per week for the 1990 and 1991 seasons.

3) *Competence:* we had to have the ability, knowledge and experience that enabled us to recognize opportunities and make the idea work.

4) *Confidence:* we needed to believe that we could make it work. This is important. Every new idea entails risk, and it takes confidence to push doubts aside and resolutely move forward in spite of the risk.

5) *Contacts:* the expression "It's not what you know that counts, but who you know" is partially true. The new Glacier Bay cruises would never have happened without our contacts with the National Park Service, financial institutions, VECO and the travel industry.

6) *Capital:* when the opportunity opened to begin new Glacier Bay cruises, we had the financial resources that enabled us to purchase the *Glacier Bay Explorer*. You can have a great idea, ability, confidence, a window of opportunity, a world of experience, and a host of influential friends; but without money in the bank, you'll never make it work. The last of the six "Cs" is the most important.

And now that I look back on it, I realize that there's a seventh "C." It is *Courage*. From the beginning my wife Marguerite stood by me faithfully, courageously supporting my efforts in every possible way. Without her steadfast support, nothing could have happened. We are now married 60 years. She has shared in the trials, tribulations, successes and failures in our business life. She has never given in to discouragement or despair. With a great deal of satisfaction and pride we both share together in our achievements.

The West Constitution — In December of 1991 I formalized my business principles into a code: basic precepts for all West Travel employees to espouse. I called it the

West Travel Constitution

- Always be guided by the highest level of honesty, integrity and fiscal responsibility.
- Oppose contributions to Political Action Committees. These are a form of political bribery. Seeking favors through monetary gifts is wrong and unprincipled.
- Do not allow gambling on our vessels. Gambling is an activity that attracts undesirable elements.
- Whenever possible, promote from within. This practice strengthens our company's morale and offers incentives to those who become permanent employees.
- Expect and demand respect from our peers in the industry and make certain that we deserve it.
- Do not be a "me-too-er." Strive always to be innovative in our operations and marketing.
- Do not take part in price wars. Our products are based on quality and service, not price. Do not be unduly influenced by what others are doing. Be original. Make decisions on what is good for us. Be aware of how we are perceived by the travel industry, travel agents, and our customers.
- Fly the American flag in all brochures and advertising and in all publicity mentioning our company. We should be proud to be American and family-owned, and proud of the reputation we have earned in the travel industry.
- Always pay our bills on time. Never be delinquent, and strive to maintain positive credit relations with our suppliers and with financial institutions.
- Show humaneness toward our suppliers and our employees. Be tolerant, understanding and fair in our treatment of all employees and customers.
- We must hold true to these principles!